NICE GIRLS CAN (MEN CAN, TOO)

PERSONAL ADS: A CAREER WOMAN'S GUIDE

*Best Wishes
Mary Hale*

by Mary Hale

Published by
TALKING HEARTS PRESS
1155 Camino del Mar #148
Del Mar, California 92014

All rights reserved. No part of this book may be reproduced or transmitted in any form or by any means, electronic or mechanical, including photocopying, recording or by any information storage and retrieval system without written permission from the author, except for the inclusion of brief quotations in a review.

Copyright © 1995 by Mary Hale

Cover design by StephGrafx, Del Mar, CA 619/792-7666

Library of Congress Number: 95-061044
ISBN: Paperback - 0-9646713-1-X

To my mother, Rose Hodgson, for her wisdom,

my children, Lenny & Ingrid Dudek, for their humor and insight

and, of course, to Richard Krygier,

my beloved and perfect life-mate.

This book is a guide to how free personal ads work and how they can be used successfully to find the perfect life-mate. It's the story of how I found my wonderful new husband, and the techniques I used in the process.

I urge you to do your own research into the personal ads and examine the content and reputation of the publishers before you place an ad. Always proceed with caution — even skepticism — and always exercise common sense. My own experience with the personal ads indicates that this is a safe and discreet process, but you must always be careful when disclosing your name, address or phone number to people you have not met or do not know well.

This text is based on my own successful experiences and therefore should be used only as a general guide to behavior and customs. It is not a guarantee. Furthermore, this text contains information current only up to the printing date.

The author and publisher, Talking Hearts Press, accepts neither liability nor responsibility for any person or entity with respect to any loss or damage caused, or alleged to be caused, directly or indirectly by the information contained in this book.

If you do not wish to be bound by the above terms, you may return this book to the publisher for a full refund.

CONTENTS

Preface VI

CHAPTER 1: A NICE GIRL LIKE ME 1

• My Story • Single in Paradise • Mr. Wonderful • How a Neighbor Convinced Me to Use the Personal Ads • The Secret of My Success • People Just Like You • Are Personal Ads for You? • Not Now •

CHAPTER 2: THE MAGIC OF PERSONAL ADS 17

• Condense Years of Searching Into Months • My Ad • The Architect • Increase the Quality of Your Contacts • Prequalify for Potential Compatibility • Initial Attraction Can Be Distracting •

CHAPTER 3: HOW FREE PERSONAL ADS WORK 29

• Free Advertising • Voice Mail Technology Makes the Difference • Private and Discreet • The Executive • Jumping on the Information Superhighway •

CHAPTER 4: ORGANIZING FOR EFFECTIVE RESULTS 37

• The Most Important Project • Keep a Journal • File System for Efficiency and Finesse • Handling Multiple Ads • The Judge •

CHAPTER 5: WHO YOU ARE, WHAT YOU WANT 49

• Identify and Describe Your Goals • Dream Sequence and Reality Check • Be Honest, Be Yourself • Worksheet to Get Started • Words That Work • What Will Not Work for You • The Chief Executive Officer •

CHAPTER 6: CREATE YOUR OWN AD 63

• Opening Lines to Get Attention • Descriptive Words to Market and Target • Specifics to Direct and Narrow Response • The Italian Stallion • Writing Your Ad • Experimenting with Different Approaches • Placing Your Ad •

CHAPTER 7: VOICE MAIL: THE REAL YOU 78
• It's Time to Get Real • Tools for Targeting Your Audience •
Mirror Effect: Tell Them About You • Plan in Advance to Sound Great • The
Dentist •

CHAPTER 8: SCREENING AND RATING YOUR CALLS 90
• It's a Fast Track • Listen for Nuances • Trust Your First Impression •
Replay Before You Erase • Summarize While It's Fresh • Red Flags •
Ranking Your Candidates • The Lawyer •

CHAPTER 9: INTERVIEWING: A UNIQUE EXPERIENCE 103
• Remember They Asked You to Call • The New Etiquette •
You're In Control • Personal Information Adds Up • The Interview •
Be Prepared to Share Similar Details • Truth, Fiction, and Embellishment •
The Engineer • Maximum Results •

CHAPTER 10: IMPORTANT RULES FOR THE FIRST MEETING 122
• Meet On Your Terms • The Perfect Place to Meet •
Signs to Watch For • Give a Gesture If Interested • Be Generous
of Heart When Disappointed • The Mistake •

CHAPTER 11: RECOGNIZING THE RIGHT MATCH FOR YOU 132
• The Four Keys to a Lasting Relationship • Give It Time •
Evaluate What Works • Chemistry May Surprise You • The Doctor •

CHAPTER 12: TO YOUR SUCCESS! 144
• The Art of the Possible • Have a Buddy for Morale and Support • Change
and Evolve Your Goals and Ad • Sally's Success • The Man of My Dreams •
If At First You Don't Succeed •

PREFACE

Despite all the differences between men and women, we share many things. We all want to find someone who loves us as much as we love them. We all want to find someone to share the good times and the bad. Someone who cares about the things we care about. Someone to make us smile. Someone we can respect and communicate with mentally, physically, emotionally and spiritually. Someone we can grow old with. A person who acknowledges and appreciates our talents and accepts our shortcomings. Someone who likes us.

The rapid pace of our society has made it more difficult than ever to find a life-mate. You can try your luck at a bar, a party, through social events or chance meetings. But do you really believe you're going to meet the love of your life in a bar or in the produce section of your local grocery store or through a blind date that your best friend set up for you?

What are the odds? At best, it could take a long time.

Why leave your future to chance? You probably take more time planning what you're going to have for dinner than you do planning to meet the man or woman of your dreams. We all lead busy and active lives — but now is the best time to take charge of your future. If you don't take the time to do this now, when will you?

I know that, when your plate is already full, you just can't imagine adding one more task to your busy schedule. However, *this is your most important task*. You simply *have* to give it the priority and attention in your life that it deserves.

In *Nice Girls Can (Men Can, Too)*, I will introduce you to the most effective and efficient way for you to find your life-mate — the personal ads. Personal ads are convenient, safe, efficient, free (usually), and fabulously successful. People from all walks of life, all over the country are using them.

Electronic voice mail technology has dramatically transformed the dating ritual. The new etiquette is to interview your prospects before you meet them. Today's personal ads take full advantage of this technology, giving you better opportunities to screen potential dates before you spend your time and energy on them.

At age forty-four, I found my second husband through the free personal ads. It wasn't until I began sharing my techniques that I realized my approach was unique in many fundamental ways. My approach was systematic and organized — business-like.

When I was active in the personal ad market, I received many messages from men. Can you imagine my reaction when I heard a woman's voice on my voice mail? She quickly said, "Please don't hang up — this is not a weird call. I am prominent in my community and recently separated. I saw your ad, your voice mail was very interesting, and I like what you are doing. I would really appreciate your help in explaining how this works and how I might use it. Please call me."

I was surprised and flattered to receive this message. The caller had recognized that my ad and voice mail approach were different, even outstanding. We agreed to meet, and she turned out to be a very attractive business woman serving on the city council of a nearby town.

As I spoke with her and others who came to me for advice, it became increasingly clear why my approach was so successful — and how it can work for others.

Since then, I have taught seminars to share my story and techniques with more people. This book has grown out of that adventure. It's a guide for success and the story of how I found my perfect lifemate. You can use this book for your personal purposes and goals.

My approach to the personal ads is naturally from a woman's perspective, but men can learn from it, too. Every technique discussed in this book will work just as well for a man as for a woman.

Perhaps you're not ready to settle down yet. Maybe you're looking for new friends, or someone to travel with. This is still a great way to meet quality people — the kind of people you want to meet. It doesn't happen by accident.

I advertised. So can you.

Mary Hale
Del Mar, California

P.S. I would love to hear your adventures, your adaptations of the personal ad process, your comments and your success stories. Please write to me in care of Talking Hearts Press, 1155 Camino Del Mar #148, Del Mar, California 92014.

CHAPTER 1

A Nice Girl Like Me

I'm a lucky woman. As I write this book, I am married to the man of my dreams. We share a charming home just steps from the beach in a small coastal town in Southern California. We often walk hand-in-hand along the shore — relaxed and happy in the comfort of our hearts, our love and our future. We both have challenging careers, and we are active socially and in our community.

We are truly living in paradise. More than just material comfort, we share and communicate on all levels.

It wasn't always this way. Only three years ago, I was a single parent of two teen-aged children. Paradise lacked just one thing — the right man to share it with, to plan a life with and enjoy!

MY STORY

My childhood was a happy one. I was born and raised in a semi-rural area twenty miles outside of Ann Arbor, Michigan. My friends and I lived carefree and modest Midwestern lives. I spent my summers sailing and swimming in the many lakes surrounding our hometown; my winters were filled with ice skating, sledding and snowball fights with the boys. Between summer and winter, I could always find a horse to borrow and a friend to ride with.

My loving parents provided me with many privileges and most of the benefits of life. Perhaps this contributed to my idealistic and simplistic understanding of life and marriage.

I married right out of college. I was twenty-one, with a degree in art and education. What did I know of life?

I suppose I married for all the wrong reasons. The intoxicating mix of adolescence, raging hormones and the urge to start a family overwhelmed me.

Alternative lifestyles were all the rage then, and my young husband and I truly believed we could live on love, brown rice and our organic garden. Our marriage wasn't a bad one, but something just wasn't right about it. Looking back, I can see that the seeds of dissatisfaction were there from our earliest days together. It was just a matter of time before those seeds germinated and grew — choking the life out of our union.

I started married life as an elementary school art teacher and, before I knew it, we had two young children — a son and a daughter — to care for. I found a creative outlet (and a source of income and recognition) exhibiting my art work at local galleries.

Eventually, we pulled up stakes and, leaving the security of our friends and family in Michigan, succumbed to the lure of sun and prosperity in the Golden State of California.

We bought a home in San Diego and planted a garden. The value of our home grew as rapidly as our plants and trees. With the children in school, I found time to pursue my artwork and enjoy volunteering for non-profit art organizations. I later parlayed my volunteer experience into a staff position as a fundraiser for the Combined Arts and Education Council of San Diego.

I was very successful raising money for the Council, but after many months of answering to a demanding board of directors, I began to ask myself what else I could do with these same skills. I decided to get into real estate.

I couldn't have picked a better time to start my real estate career. The economy was booming, home prices were appreciating rapidly and people had the income to buy expensive houses. I also had the good fortune to join the best real estate brokerage in the area. The training was fabulous, and I made a lot of money.

This was an exciting time for us. With the unbelievable equity from our first California property, along with our combined incomes, we bought our dream home. And it was a dream, custom-built on two acres high atop a hill with panoramic views of the Pacific Ocean.

The beginning of the end of my marriage came when my husband decided to go into real estate sales. Soon after he followed me into the profession, the real estate market began a downward slump. The nation went into a recession, and Southern California property values rapidly declined. The world around us went into a stressful economic period and so, too, did our relationship.

Prosperity turned into a negative cash flow, and our marriage was put to the test. My income alone was not enough to pay the bills. I watched as our resources dwindled. First to go was the IRA, then the stocks. When my husband put a line of credit on our home equal to its equity, I knew that soon there would be very little money left.

Seventeen years earlier, we had promised that we would honor each other in sickness and health, through the good times and the bad. Now the good times were becoming a distant memory, and the bad times began to dominate our relationship.

I could see the writing on the wall. We were about to lose our home and everything we had spent years working to achieve. I listed the house for sale, hoping to motivate my husband to take some action. Our beautiful garden had become overgrown and choked with weeds.

The situation might not have shaken a strong marriage, but it forever diminished my respect for this kind man and good father. I felt that, to save my children and myself from certain financial ruin, I would have to take action. It was all up to me.

When our home sold, I filed for divorce.

CHAPTER 1: A NICE GIRL LIKE ME

SINGLE IN PARADISE

There I was, single in paradise. I had managed to avoid being pulled into a dark financial abyss created by my spouse, but I was on my own now. I purchased a condo near the beach in the best school district. I could no longer depend on my husband to help keep my family together. The fortunes of my children and myself — the ups and the downs — would depend on my ability to recover from this great upheaval. I had no choice but to accept the responsibility and begin to create a new — perhaps even better — life.

It took time, and I confess that I had many fears. I was afraid of being alone. Afraid that I wouldn't be able to make enough money to pay the bills to keep my family above water. Afraid that I would never find someone to share my life with. Afraid of growing old alone.

I dealt with my fears the only way I knew how — confronting them and facing them one by one. I studied. I researched. I went to seminars. I must have read every book in the self-help section of the local bookstore, looking for guidance and information to assist me in creating the new life I dreamed of. I even went to a psychic. I left no possible source of information untouched in my search for answers.

For me, being single was like studying a foreign language. I took it one step at a time.

Slowly but surely, I regained my confidence. As I did, I began to emerge from the nest I had built for my children and myself. My first steps were tiny, baby steps. Fortunately, I had my career, and I had managed to get my household on an even keel. I received a lot of support from many dear friends.

I never had to worry about finding something to do. My event calendar was full of gallery openings and community projects. I was even appointed to a countywide arts council by our county supervisor.

A year after my divorce, I began to meet men and consider dating again. This, however, was not a comfortable transition. It had been

CHAPTER 1: A NICE GIRL LIKE ME

twenty years since I had dated — or even thought about the possibility of sharing my life and love with anyone other than my husband. In that time, I had forgotten what it was like to date. I had no idea how to behave.

I had put many of my emotions into cold storage during the trauma of my divorce and establishing my own identity as a single parent. By this time, those emotions were as frozen as the icicles that used to cling to the eaves of my childhood home in Michigan.

In the beginning, I did everything possible to avoid situations that might lead to a date. I was in a real quandary. I knew I wanted to enjoy the companionship of a man, but I couldn't bring myself to follow through on this desire. My body began to say "maybe," but my brain was still saying "no, not yet." I don't know if I was afraid of rejection, or just the unknown. I had many opportunities to enter the world of dating, but I simply wasn't ready.

About this time, an acquaintance who was a former naval officer, pilot and Annapolis graduate, a real-life officer and gentleman, phoned me at the office to ask me out for dinner. I was taken totally off guard. Not knowing what to do — and practically in shock — I said no. Getting off the phone, I was physically shaking. I regretted my impulsive "no" almost immediately. He would have been a great first date, and an easy, small step forward.

I met several nice men in the conventional ways — through my work, through mutual friends or at one of the many social events that filled my busy life.

I also had Beth. She became my leader in the single life and, later, my partner in using the personal ads. Beth has been a great asset and door opener. She's the kind of person who instinctively knows how, where and when to do things to meet other single people. I was luckier than most; I had Beth as a tour guide.

In addition to being smart and fun, Beth is beautiful. What a treat to let her lead the way, striking up conversations and then introducing me to her new acquaintances. We made quite a team, and together we turned a lot of heads. This was definitely amusing, but neither of us was meeting the kind of men we really wanted to meet.

MR. WONDERFUL

Then I met Mr. Wonderful. A girl in my office asked me who I'd like to go out with. I named a gentleman we both knew through work. We had mutual friends, and I knew some of the women he dated. Taking my cue, this co-worker spoke to my dream date, suggesting that he ask me out.

Mr. Wonderful and I spent many great times together — dinners out, concerts and other special events. It was a real treat to do the things that I hadn't had time to do while I was raising my children. Although he was not particularly affluent, Mr. Wonderful had a real flair for enjoying life. He was the first man I really cared about since my divorce. I began to envision a life for us.

A savvy bachelor, he recognized the stars in my eyes, and told me not to anticipate a future together — that he would never marry. I was crushed!

This was not so wonderful.

Next, I was introduced to Mr. Drop Dead Wrong Man. He was the proverbial "bad boy." I knew of his reputation long before I ever met him. It's not that he was a playboy or ladies' man — he wasn't. He just marched to his own drummer.

Eccentric, and very, very wealthy, Mr. Drop Dead Wrong Man was as comfortable and confident riding his polo ponies as he was sweeping me off my feet. We had major chemistry, and we spent a lot of time together. He had been divorced for seven years, and I began to believe in Beth's assessment that he was probably ready to settle down.

He wasn't. And, although I was disappointed, I knew that I

wouldn't be happy with a man who wasn't willing to commit.

There is something in a woman — in me — that looks to the future and wants commitment. Fortunately, there are many men who also long for a life-mate they can treasure. But where were they?

Finally, I met Mr. Perfect Professor. Introduced to me by mutual friends, Mr. Perfect Professor was a successful designer who taught at a local college. He seemed perfect! Attractive, healthy, trim, well-dressed, educated — my friends had done their homework this time. We became good friends and quickly became an item on the local social scene. I really enjoyed this man — he was even a great cook. Unfortunately, although we shared many common interests, there was absolutely no chemistry.

Fate seemed very cruel, but I learned something from each of these men. There were aspects of each that were special to me. These glimpses of life's possibilities only reminded me how nice it would be to find a man who was a keeper. (*Keeper* was the slang expression Beth and I used to evaluate the men we met. If someone had a lot of interest in us and had qualities we believed would make him worth investing our time in, then he was a *keeper*.)

I had first met men I viewed as keepers, but who did not view me as a long-term partner. Then I met a man who was a perfect companion and who had potential for settling down — a definite keeper — but there was no spark between us. Finding a man I could care for was a slow and somewhat painful process, but I was learning what worked and what didn't work for me.

I enjoyed the time I spent with Mr. Wonderful, Mr. Drop Dead Wrong Man and Mr. Perfect Professor, but I came to the realization that it was taking far too long to find out whether or not my dates were long-term prospects. By the time I found out, I had already invested weeks and even months — and far too much emotion — learning that we would not share a future together. I knew that there must be a man

— the one man — out there for me. One I could enjoy and share similar goals with, including marriage.

These close encounters and near-misses left me bruised but wiser — and still optimistic. I now had a better idea of what I was looking for in a relationship, and what would really last.

HOW A NEIGHBOR CONVINCED ME TO USE THE PERSONAL ADS

Although I hadn't lost hope, I wasn't very inspired by my first baby steps into the world of dating. No one encouraged me — my mother tied her hopes to the idea that perhaps an older man would be interested! As busy as I was with my career, my family and my social calendar, I just wasn't meeting very many eligible men of quality — men also looking for a traditional relationship. The ones I met were, for one reason or another, unable to commit to a long-term relationship. I knew there must be some better way to find my life mate. I just didn't know what that better way was.

My neighbor Joe often listened to my tales of hurt feelings and misunderstandings. Joe and I worked closely together to produce a local TV program. While meeting to discuss our show, the conversation often turned to our personal lives. I was always interested in getting Joe's opinion, insight and masculine perspective. I valued his advice highly.

Joe let me in on a secret that he successfully used to find quality women to date — the personal ads.

It's not that I was unaware of the personal ads. It's just that I had never imagined that a "nice girl" like me could use them to find the kind of nice guy I was looking for. I always thought of the personals as a place where desperate people went looking for other losers. Joe convinced me that this wasn't the case. Indeed, he had found fabulous women using the personal ads.

After retiring from a successful career in New York, Joe settled in

Del Mar and quickly became active with his temple, local Democratic politics and many other groups. For all that, he was not meeting eligible women. Looking at Joe, you wouldn't suspect that he would attract the quality of women that he does. While he is a wonderful man, he doesn't exactly have movie-star looks. However, using personal ads and voice mail, he has met and dated many accomplished and wonderful women — the kind of women he was looking for.

He explained the personal ads process and how they really work. I had no idea where to begin until Joe showed me. Through his example, I learned that the ads are discreet and effective and, with a little work, I could find the kind of man I was looking for. He convinced me that quality people use the personal ads. All I had to do was let them know that I was looking for them.

Even with Joe's encouragement, I didn't expect the personal ads to be such a huge success. I quickly began meeting many great men. Soon Beth started using the ads with me, and together we embarked on a search that was a lot of fun and very enlightening. We learned as we went along, and improved our skills considerably over the many months that we used the personal ads together.

It took me two years to find the love of my life through the personal ads. During that time I learned a lot, and I met many wonderful men.

THE SECRET OF MY SUCCESS

Instinctively, I applied business skills to the search process, to make the best use of my time and increase my opportunities. It was just a natural approach for me — they were much the same techniques that I used with my clients. In real estate, we always want to know what the clients' needs are, what their time-frame is, and whether they have the financial resources to follow through. This makes obvious sense in business, and it made sense in my personal life, too.

CHAPTER 1: A NICE GIRL LIKE ME

Gearing my business skills towards the personal ads was automatic. Later, I realized that this was exactly why I was so successful.

I have written this book to give you the benefit of the skills I developed, skills that can help shorten your search for your life-mate. They can help you embark on an effective new way to meet quality people — men and women who meet your needs and goals.

While personal ads have been around for a long time, voice mail technology has only recently been available. In the past, if you wanted to respond to a personal ad, you had to endure a cumbersome process of writing letters to a post office box which would then be forwarded to the advertiser (a system that could add precious weeks to the process).

Voice mail has done away with all that.

Now, your prospect — attracted by your ad — can call your voice mailbox and leave a message for you moments after they read your ad. They don't know who you are — they just know your voice mail number. You can retrieve messages from your voice mailbox anytime you desire, from any place you desire. If you are interested, you can call your prospect back immediately, or whenever you choose. By interviewing your prospects on the phone, you get a great head start on who they are and what they are looking for; then you decide whether or not you wish to meet.

This book will demystify the process of using personal ads and show you that there is nothing to be afraid of — you will actually have fun as you search for your life-mate.

If you haven't checked out the personal ads in your local paper lately, take a look. Although most publications have sensational ads that imply kinky, even sordid encounters, don't let this put you off. These distasteful ads tend to be the ones that catch your eye first, and they give personals the mixed reputation that they have. Learn to look past them at the other ads. There are all kinds! In fact, most ads

CHAPTER 1: A NICE GIRL LIKE ME

are from people like you and me. People who are hardworking, educated, and who share a desire to meet someone special.

If you aren't ready to settle down yet, you can use the personal ads to find new friends and companions. Or you can target your market and screen your results to find someone to love and spend the rest of your life with.

PEOPLE JUST LIKE YOU

What is your picture of people who advertise in the personal ads? Do you see them as winners? As losers? Old? Young? Risk takers? Boring? Desperate? Promiscuous? Socially inadequate, outcasts, rejects?

All kinds of people place personal ads. And all kinds of people respond to personal ads. Despite popular belief, there is no one "type" of person who uses the personal ads. Instead, there is a tremendous diversity. Here are a few sample ads to give you an idea of what to expect:

REWARD OFFERED for information leading to romantic arrest of an elusive, exceptionally tall/trim, refined cutie pie considered embraceably disarming. Creative genius (6'3" eligible bachelor), hilltop mansion; be committed to loving pets/gardening. Serious reward offered!

CULTURED, CLASSY, attractive, blonde. Interests include travel, theatre, jazz. Seeks tall, financially secure professional, gentleman, 42-55 for long term.

ATTRACTIVE, AFROCENTRIC, educated, down-to-earth black female, 26, looking for same in tall, adventurous, non-smoking black male, 26-36. No games would be greatly appreciated.

"GREAT LOOKING" ITALIAN, 48, secure, easy-going, giving, affectionate, non-smoker, great shape. Seeking fit, honest, sincere, loyal lady to enjoy life, be 1st in my life.

As you can see, you can expect to meet all sorts of fun and interesting people through the personal ads. By no means the haunt of those seeking a one-night stand, personal ads are a respectable and essential way to locate, meet, and date high-quality partners.

ARE PERSONAL ADS FOR YOU?

You've read my story. You know I'm not a loser or weirdo or crazy person. I'm not even a hopeless romantic. What I am is practical. I'm an ordinary person who realizes how short life is. I knew I wanted a companion and lover, and at forty-two I couldn't afford years and years of searching and disappointment.

I found a reasonable, realistic, functional way to meet the people I wanted to meet, to narrow the field to those with the same hopes and dreams I had. Using the same techniques, you can do it, too.

By now, I know some of you are convinced that it will be worth your while to give the personal ads a try. You've had at least one good example (me!) of how personal ads can increase the quantity and quality of the people you meet, eliminating the hit-and-miss of chance encounters while multiplying the effectiveness of your search for your life mate by many times. In later chapters, you will begin to get a feel for the ease of use, the control and the security that using personal ads gives you.

However, I also know that some of you aren't sure yet. You may be curious but, for one reason or another, you're not ready to commit. In teaching people how to get the most out of the personal ads, I have discovered that, if my students have any concerns about using personal ads, three questions in particular tend to dominate. This is very important. Before you embark on this journey, it is critical that we resolve these issues so that you will be ready to commit yourself to this process wholeheartedly.

Let's take the time to address these concerns one by one:

Are personal ads safe? In my years of experience with personal ads, I have found them to be a very safe way to meet the kind of people I wanted to meet. I firmly believe, and my research indicates, that anyone who exercises a little judgment and common sense can use personal ads with confidence and without fear of personal harm.

At every seminar I lead on this subject, I am asked, "Aren't there a lot of wackos out there responding to personal ads?" In my experience, the answer is a clear and vocal "No!" Personal ads just don't offer the kind of immediate gratification that most of the sickos we read about in the newspapers seem to crave. However, this is not a blanket guarantee. You still have to exercise caution and normal common sense!

Are personal ads discreet? I can't imagine a more discreet way to meet someone new. Your name and number do not appear in your ad, or even in your voice mail message.

Think about it. *You* place the ad. *You* record the voice mail message in the privacy of your own home or office. *You* listen to the messages that your callers leave and *you* decide whether you will call them back. If you do call them back and you don't like what you hear, then you can graciously say good-bye *without the caller ever knowing who you are, where you live, or what your phone number is.* You have control of the entire process.

The kind of people I want to meet don't use personal ads. This could not be further from the truth. Personal ads today are used by people from all walks of life, from minimum-wage workers to the rich and famous (or at least, the near-rich and famous). It is my experience that the people who tend to use personal ads are hard-working, educated, ambitious, career-oriented people who just don't have the time, opportunity, or inclination to spend hanging out at bars or attending singles functions. Aren't these the kind of busy, goal-oriented people you would like to meet?

Who wouldn't?

NOT NOW

Few women plan to be single — it just happens.

My goal was to remarry, but only if I could find the right man. I knew the compromising one goes through — consciously and unconsciously — trying to keep a bad relationship together. I promised myself that I would never allow myself to make those compromises ever again.

I was willing to face the prospect that I might never marry again. I planned to continue to succeed with my career, to be financially responsible and to be prepared for old age — alone, if need be. I knew very well that, if I was self-sufficient, marriage would be an option and not a necessity.

This is so important! I have seen far too many women refuse to face reality. You must be fiscally responsible. You have to take care of yourself. While attractive clothes are certainly an asset in attracting men, you must still watch out for the bottom line. Very few men these days are looking to be the sole means of financial support for a woman.

If you have your own life, your own career and your own financial resources, you are much more powerful and in a much better position to negotiate your future than if you are financially unstable and weak. If your idea of financial planning is to buy lottery tickets, it's time to start your nest egg — however modest to begin with.

Another misconception is that you have to be gorgeous to land the man of your dreams. This is simply not true! Many women spend

CHAPTER 1: A NICE GIRL LIKE ME

large sums of money on cosmetic surgery. And for what?

Without a doubt, it is important to be attractive. Just attractive. The most famous courtesans of history and many of the women who won the hearts of important men were not exceptionally good looking. They were clever, well-informed, gracious and intriguing. Beauty was rarely their most outstanding accomplishment.

So be attractive, be well groomed and, of course, dress well — but then get on with your life.

If you're waiting until you lose weight before you start your personal ad campaign, there are two possibilities — and this goes for both men and women. One, you are being too hard on yourself, and you need to learn to accept yourself for who you are and get going. Two, you really do need to lose some weight. If that's the case, what is your goal weight?

Most likely, your ideal weight is a vague memory of how good you looked when you were eighteen years old, or when you were twenty-five or thirty. I'm sorry to burst your bubble, but none of us is getting any younger. It's highly unlikely that you are going to ever look like you did when you were eighteen. If your ideal goal is to lose thirty-five pounds, wouldn't fifteen pounds be easier, and still a significant benefit to you? Stop making yourself nuts and just get started.

What's the best way to lose weight? There are many ways to lose weight, and the rewards are genuine. Don't try to do it all at once. You have to factor in the occasional treat. Understand that, if you are serious about losing weight, you will probably have to adopt some lifestyle changes such as increased exercise into your schedule.

Even small changes can make a difference. To start, be realistic. Personally, I need exercise to burn calories. If I'm not exercising, then no cookies or desserts! I hate organized activities or anything that has to be scheduled in advance, that requires driving to get there or, worse yet, a fee. Because of this, I narrowed my options down to three: walk for an hour, bike thirty minutes, or swim. I found I could do one of these exercises at least three times a week. The results are apparent. You can do it, too.

There are as many excuses for not taking action now as there are stars in the sky. N*ot now* because I'm too busy. N*ot now* because I'm too tired. N*ot now* because I'm too old. N*ot now* because I'm overweight.

You can always think up excuses for not doing something. However, finding your life-mate is too important a task to leave to chance. You've got to throw your excuses out the window and just do it! If not now — when?

In the next chapter, we will explore the advantages of personal ads in detail. Sure, you can still meet people the old-fashioned way — by chance. Many fine relationships are the result of pure happenstance. But, as you will see, personal ads provide you with the opportunity to conduct a focused and accelerated search for your life mate — a process that you control and direct according to your rules.

Personal ads can help you reach your goals. After all, aren't your goals important?

CHAPTER 2

The Magic of Personal Ads

The truth is, men want to meet women, and women want to meet men. Traditionally, this arrangement has worked out pretty well. However, no matter how many groups you join, how many friends you network with, how many classes you take, meeting men and women you might be willing to spend the rest of your life with can be very much a hit-and-miss affair.

Have you ever caught someone's glance at the airport, shopping mall, movie theatre, or at an event you're attending? Perhaps you feel a spark of interest on their part, a brief connection, a fleeting attraction. Although you don't know the other person, you sense or imagine that you may have some potential together.

The personal ads bring these unknown people and others just like them into your life as candidates you can meet. The only difference is that, with personal ads, you don't see them first. You become acquainted over the phone and later decide if you wish to meet in person and see if you find those same sparks.

Using the personal ads, you take the hit-and-miss out the process, and you target exactly the people you want to attract. You can form friendships, you can date and you can marry, if that's what you want.

You've probably seen advertisements for personal dating services that claim guaranteed results and promise they will only introduce you to eligible singles specifically selected for you. Some include personality tests, questionnaires, even videotapes. It's not uncommon for these placement services to charge up to $20,000.

CHAPTER 2: THE MAGIC OF PERSONAL ADS

Even if you have that kind of money to spend, and are willing to go to the dating service's offices every week to review photos and videos, will the results justify the expense? I believe you can do a better job of screening potential mates for yourself than any service can. It will take time and some effort, but it is virtually free.

The million dollar questions are: How can you increase the number of opportunities available to you? How can you improve the quality of your opportunities? And, finally, how can you speed up the process and make it work faster than traditional ways of meeting people?

CONDENSE YEARS OF SEARCHING INTO MONTHS

If you meet people the usual way, it can take years to find someone you might be willing to spend the rest of your life with. Let's face it, you can use the old friend-of-a-friend technique for years and still not find the right person for you.

What you need is a way to speed up the process. Instead of meeting one prospect a month, wouldn't it be great if you could meet, say, five or ten prospects a week?

Personal ads do just that. Depending on how you write your ad and what you say in your voice mail message, you will have more prospects than you will know what to do with. Sure, some of them will be out in left field, but I believe you will be pleasantly surprised at how many calls you receive from sincere, thoughtful and interesting people.

I, of course, was the classic over-achiever. I often had up to four ads running at the same time. I received lots of calls. Believe me when I say that personal ads can provide you with more quality opportunities than you could ever imagine possible.

By providing you with a much larger pool of potential mates — people who have read your ad, listened to your voice mail, who know what you're looking for and who are very interested in meeting you —

you can review the qualifications of many more people than you ever could through chance meetings. Your ability to review and interview a larger pool of prospects means that you will find qualified individuals much faster than you would any other way. This process can condense three years of chance encounters into six months of focused meetings.

MY AD

My friend and neighbor Joe did me a great favor — he wrote my first ad. It was a great ad. In fact, it turned out to be so successful that I re-ran it many times during the course of my search. I know that you must be curious by now, so here it is:

DYNAMIC BLOND PETITE. Independent, North Coastal business woman, talk show host/personality, happy, healthy, active, seeks gentleman, aged 45-50, for potential relationship.

This ad attracted a lot of attention. Of course, that is exactly what I wanted. The key to success with personal ads is to initially create as many opportunities for yourself as you can. There will be plenty of time later in the process to select out the prospects who do not meet your criteria. At the beginning of the process, it is better to have too many opportunities to choose from than not enough.

Big companies like AT&T, General Motors and Procter & Gamble spend millions of dollars each year to advertise their products. They advertise *to maximize their opportunities*. Each one of these firms has great products to sell, but if a potential buyer doesn't know the product exists, they can't respond.

Advertising informs the public that a product is there to buy and explains what the product has to offer. How long do you think it would take for McDonald's to go out of business if they didn't repeatedly

CHAPTER 2: THE MAGIC OF PERSONAL ADS

advertise their products? If people don't know about a product – or don't remember it – they won't go out of their way to buy it.

In much the same way, you can use personal ads to increase your opportunities. Any salesperson will tell you that marketing is a numbers game. In real estate, if you want to sell a home, you have got to get the opportunity in front of as many qualified buyers as possible. You have to place so many ads, make so many phone calls or hold an open house for exposure. If one hundred people are given an opportunity, you are far more likely to sell the property than if you only present ten people with the opportunity.

It's the same thing when you market yourself. Think of every contact with an eligible prospect as an opportunity to market and promote yourself. Personal ads allow you to present the opportunity (you!) to hundreds, even thousands, of prospects. Not only can they read your ad but, using voice mail, they can listen to you talk about your likes, your dislikes and the kind of person you are looking for.

To get an idea of exactly the amount of exposure personal ads offer, I interviewed employees at the two largest newspapers in my area – one a daily, the other a weekly. It's clear that the popularity of personal ads has skyrocketed. According to the management at the local daily newspaper, the *San Diego Union-Tribune*, they have approximately twelve hundred ads in publication at any given time, and they receive four to five hundred new ads every week. Now, here's the interesting part. Many ads receive up to two hundred calls.

That is not a misprint. *Two hundred calls*. To be sure, many ads receive less, but just think of the possibilities!

My own ad response varied from nine to thirty calls per week, occasionally more. I never received two hundred messages because my ad was specific for age preference and other parameters. Still, thirty calls are a lot to review and consider. And my prospects were terrific.

Where else can you get that kind of exposure?

THE ARCHITECT

The day I received his voice mail message, there were also several others. They sounded okay, but when I got his message, my heart soared. His voice was deep and melodious. I immediately recognized his name — that of a prominent local architect. It's funny what a small world it really is. I had seen him give a presentation to a design review board I attended. I was attracted to him at that meeting, and found myself wondering if he was available and how I might meet him.

Tall, handsome, obviously nice, and smart. I eagerly returned his call. I already knew I wanted to meet him. He suggested lunch and I jumped at the opportunity. Lunch was fabulous — our conversation was sparkling and friendly. I learned that he liked long hikes in remote areas and that he had been married twice before. The last marriage had been brief but, even when he knew the marriage was on the rocks, he had agreed to adopt a baby girl.

That was the first sign I had that perhaps his judgment was not as good as it could be, at least in my opinion. We enjoyed lunch, then went for a walk. We talked of seeing a movie together soon.

When he called back, he suggested that I stop by his home to meet his daughter. Now, one of the things I was looking for was a man without children. I knew how difficult that would be — most of the men in the age group I was targeting had already been married at least once, and many had children. I already had two teenagers, and I just didn't want to confuse the issue by adding new children to our family.

I got along beautifully with the architect's charming two-and-a-half-year-old daughter. Even so, I was eager to leave when I could!

He called me again, but we never did see that movie we talked about. The spark just wasn't there for me. Hiking sounded dull. His home was boring — the decor was dull and there wasn't anything for me to get interested in.

Later, I introduced him to a friend who likes to hike and adores young children. They were a match made in heaven.

Although we didn't hit it off, I was encouraged by this close encounter. I had met a handsome and successful man — through the personal ads! I knew I was on to something here. I couldn't wait to see if there were any new messages in my voice mailbox!

Who knows, the next call might be the man of my dreams...

INCREASE THE QUALITY OF YOUR CONTACTS

We all know that it's far too easy to meet the wrong people. How many times have you dated someone only to find out there was some fundamental problem or incompatibility in your budding relationship? It could be something as minor as the fact that you love classical music and they hate it. It could be something much more serious — like they are married and looking for nothing more than a fling.

Personal ads can increase the quality of the people that you meet. We all want to meet quality people — and the personal ads are uniquely positioned to help you do that. Although personal ad publications attract a wide variety of people, most attract a high percentage of top achievers — busy, confident people. Think about it for a moment and you'll understand why. If you sincerely want to get something out of the personal ads, you have to be willing to put in the small amount of effort required to succeed.

You may be surprised that, when you mention the personal ads, others around you will chime in with a success story of their own or friends they know who met and married through the personal ads. The receptionist at my dentist's office had a great story to share with me about her girlfriend who found success through the personals.

As the host of a local TV show, I meet all sorts of interesting and prominent people. While I was writing this book, one of my guests was Jim Cameron, founder of the Journalism Forum on a major on-line computer network. Jim had a dynamic career with NBC News, and he won numerous journalism awards before he launched his computer service. You will never meet a nicer, brighter, more interesting and energetic gentleman.

Jim readily told me that he met his wife of five years through the personal ads.

You will see as you read this book that I met a lot of quality men as a result of the personal ads — men I probably wouldn't have met otherwise. An architect, lawyers, engineers, doctors, dentists, a judge, executives, and a CEO or two. Where else could you meet eligible prospects of this quality? It's a fabulous opportunity, and it's basically free.

PREQUALIFY FOR POTENTIAL COMPATIBILITY

One of the keys to increasing the quality of your opportunities is the ability to prequalify your prospects before you agree to meet. This is standard operating procedure in real estate. We always want to know in advance what our clients want, as well as their ability to commit and time frame, before we waste a lot of effort. Here's how it works in the personal ads.

Through your ad, you give your prospects some idea of who you are. This is the first level of prequalification. If, for example, you say you're a redhead, men who are looking for blondes or brunettes will go on to the next ad — they screen themselves out. Next, your voice mail message provides more detailed information about who you are and what you are looking for in a prospect. After hearing your voice mail message, a few more individuals will drop out.

If they are still interested after hearing your voice mail message, they will leave a message for you. Based on this information, you decide if the prospect meets your criteria. If he doesn't, you simply go on to the next message. If he does, you reach the final step in the prequalification process — the interview. When you call your prospect back, you can ask further, personal questions to determine if you want to meet.

I wrote the following ad for a dear friend of mine. She is one of the nicest, sweetest women in the world, but she's not fabulously attractive. I think she's beautiful, of course, because I see her inner beauty. But we couldn't come out with "stunning redhead" because she's not stunning. She's just a really neat lady.

Her ad read:

POLISH-ITALIAN girl-next-door, successful executive. Warm-hearted, loves to cook, age 43, fit but not skinny, seeking life partner.

That's all accurate. Starting out with Polish-Italian was a bit of a gamble, but we figured that some people are going to drop out right then.

That's the reason you want to prequalify your prospects. If they, for whatever reason, are not interested in a person like you, then let them drop out — you don't want to meet them anyway.

It was important to Joanne (not her real name), and it tells you something about her — that she's a normal person.

We followed this theme on her voice mail, saying,

Hello, this is Joanne. I mentioned that I'm Polish and Italian because both have influenced my cooking. I love to cook and entertain friends in my home. And I have wonderful friends. In fact, I have many of the blessings in life. I have an extremely successful career managing a local company, I've worked hard for my success, I'm

happy, physically active and, of course, healthy. I really do have almost all the joys of life. My goal is to have a partner that I can share my life with. Please leave a message and indicate the best time to call.

Doesn't that tell you something? Actually, my friend is the vice president of a company. She's one of the most successful young women I know (young meaning in her early 40s). Where is a person like this going to meet the right kind of companion? She's looking for someone who likes people, someone nice.

The person she wants to meet has a work ethic — which is why we put certain buzzwords in her voice mail. "I've worked hard for my success." "I like to entertain friends in my home."

This is a fantastic way to start screening our audience. Tell them about yourself.

It doesn't always work. The wrong people will still leave you messages. Sometimes you have to wonder, why are they wasting your time and their money to leave you ridiculous messages? I'm pretty sure I know the answer. People are optimists. They think, "Maybe I'll be the exception."

I received a message from a man whose voice was absolutely ancient — he sounded as though he had to have a white beard. Although my ad clearly indicated an age range, he still left me a lengthy message. It turned out that he spent half the year in Arizona and half the year in California. He had a mobile home in Arizona and a travel trailer here.

Be still my heart.

You just have to screen those messages out yourself. I never called him back.

Now, here's a real optimist for you. A man kept leaving me messages, and I never returned them. I don't remember why, but no matter how often he called, his messages weren't appealing. Finally, he contacted the newspaper and convinced them that there had to be something wrong with their voice mail system because I had not returned his calls.

Newspapers are very judicious about not revealing names and phone numbers — you get a written agreement when you submit your ad that it's private. So, although the newspaper would not give the man my name and number, he persisted until they agreed to mail me a note from him.

I received their business envelope and opened it to find a nice typewritten letter from someone in the personal ad department. The letter said, "Please excuse this intrusion, but this gentleman has contacted us. He feels certain that you have not received his messages. We would not give him your name and number, but we agreed to enclose this note."

Inside the envelope was a torn piece of yellow paper, wrinkly, with a just barely decipherable message asking me to call him.

So, sometimes inappropriate people will call, and they're tenacious — but they're just optimists. They're thinking, "If she's half the things she said in the ad, I would really like to have a shot at this. I'm going to give it a try."

Although they are welcome to give it a try, you don't have to be dumb enough to call them back. Bless their hearts for calling you, but you get to choose who to call.

Be selective. Remember, you're the one who's in control of this process.

INITIAL ATTRACTION CAN BE DISTRACTING

There is nothing more intoxicating than the first rush of new romance. Alcohol can't do it. Drugs aren't even close. Your heart quickens. Your pulse increases. You are transported to a special level of awareness — a place only those who have experienced the compelling power of romantic attraction know.

Unfortunately, while the pleasure of chemistry can be truly delicious, these tremendous waves of emotional intensity can interfere with your good judgment and distract you from your true goals.

Research scientists have confirmed that sexual chemistry — the sudden rush of feelings that you experience when you are with someone special — is very real. You don't even have to know the other person for the chemistry to go to work. Sometimes just being close to someone you are attracted to is enough to trigger the onrush of hormones and feelings.

Some years ago, I attended a series of management meetings for my employer — a large, national retailer. After very few of these meetings, I became acquainted with a manager from another location. Outside of our jobs, we had absolutely nothing in common. Even so, I enjoyed his sense of humor. His physical presence became very exciting to me. Fortunately, nothing ever came of our relationship — except some sincere flirting, and his offer to promptly help me when I needed to transfer an item from another store.

If you do find someone at work, at a bar or through a friend, chemistry often kicks in. If there's any attraction at all, away you go. Six weeks, six months — even six years — later, you wake up one morning to discover that your partner is not a suitable life-mate. It might be fun, it might be entertaining, but it's just not going to work over the long haul.

The personal ads allow you to step back and size up your prospect — objectively and unemotionally — before you meet and the chemistry between you goes to work.

The key to ensuring that you are objective in your search is to set clear standards and goals before you place your ad and start receiving calls. Are you going to limit your search to certain neighborhoods or telephone prefixes? Do your prospects have to be professionals, such as lawyers or doctors, or do you want to limit your search to business executives, artists or intellectuals? What if they have children? What if their children are very young? Will that make a difference?

Maybe you really aren't sure what qualities you are looking for in a partner. If that's the case, you're in luck — the personal ads can help you narrow your search and learn about yourself in the process. Once you have met a few people you definitely have nothing in common with and have no interest in, you will be better able to describe the kind of person you are seeking. Conversely, you will learn to emphasize the qualities in yourself that you want to see reflected in your prospects.

We have discussed the advantages of using personal ads over relying on the old-fashioned ways of meeting and dating other people — and even over modern, computerized inroduction services. Now it's time to learn exactly how personal ads work. In the next chapter, we will do just that.

CHAPTER 3

How Free Personal Ads Work

If you have never used the personal ads before, they can seem intimidating. I know, because I was once in your shoes. I had a lot of questions, and I wanted a lot of answers before I placed my first ad.

I firmly believe that we choose to be where we are. You may not remember making a choice — often they're made by default. If you don't take action to move forward, you are choosing by default to stay where you are.

Is it your choice to be a spectator in life, to take whatever comes to you? Or will you take action, ask for what you want and work toward a richer, fuller future?

Believe in yourself. Looks are not the issue. Who you are inside is what really counts. There will always be people who don't like the way you look. Fine. Keep advertising until you find someone who likes you just the way you are.

Finding that person, then being with them, is the greatest reward and finest pleasure in life. And you get to enjoy it every day. I decided to make the effort, to stick my neck out, to direct my energy toward finding the love of my life. It all started with that first ad — and I'm very glad I had an ad running the week Richard decided to give the personal ads a try, too.

It's actually quite easy to place your very own personal ad. You have already taken the first step — you are reading this book. I will guide you through the personal ad process. Before we are done, you will know all there is to know about how personal ads work and how to make them work for you.

CHAPTER 3: HOW FREE PERSONAL ADS WORK

FREE ADVERTISING

Just think. You can get your opportunity in front of hundreds — even thousands — of prospects for free. Here's how it works.

Personal ads are big business. You might ask how the publications make any money if it doesn't cost anything to place an ad. Indeed, if that's all there was to the process, most publications wouldn't bother. However, placing the ad is just half of the equation. The secret is that they don't make any money by running the ad — but they make tons of money from the people who call to listen to the voice mail messages, often to the tune of a dollar or more a minute.

Let's go back to that large, local daily that carries about twelve hundred ads at any given time. Don't forget that, according to the newspaper, each ad gets up to two hundred calls a week. For purposes of our discussion, let's assume twelve hundred ads a week (not a day), with a conservative average response — say fifty. That's *sixty thousand* phone calls every week.

Here's where the money is made. When you place an ad, the publisher provides you with free voice mail service and puts a four-digit number at the end of your copy. In order to respond to your ad, the reader calls the 900 number and the extension listed on your ad and listens to your voice mail. If they like what they hear, they can leave a message for you.

These ads are so successful that many publishers now offer advance credit for people who are not able to access 900 numbers from work. Potential callers use their credit cards to set up lines of credit with the publisher. Some even show up in person and pay cash for the privilege!

The two largest local publications in my area charge the caller $1.98 for the first minute and $.98 for each minute thereafter. It takes at least a couple of minutes to listen and respond. When you multiply that by sixty thousand calls, it comes to a healthy profit.

The best part is, when you place an ad, you get the benefit — for free!

CHAPTER 3: HOW FREE PERSONAL ADS WORK

There is no charge for listening to the messages left on your voice mail, no matter how many and no matter how long.

Just a note: Some specialized publications do charge a fee to run an ad. Large cities may have numerous publications offering personal ads — some free, others for a fee. In these situations, it becomes increasingly important to be familiar with the publications, to know if they are attracting the kind of people you wish to meet.

Some publications are able to charge fees for their ads because of the desirable audience they reach. *New York Magazine* currently charges $34.50 per line with a two-line minimum. Judging from the size of the ads, many people are spending $140 or more for an ad because they believe it has the potential to reach the right audience.

Free ads are definitely the best opportunity for most people. If you live near a metropolitan area, there are probably several sources for quality free ads. Keep your eye out for publications that carry personal ads. You might wish to experiment with large and small newspapers, magazines and specialty publications. Many church newsletters are even adding personals to their publication.

Any publication that caters only to sexy, kinky ads is probably not the place for a nice person like you. However, don't be put off by a publication just because it carries provocative, risqué or questionable personal ads. Some people are admittedly looking for relationships that are outside the norm. Just skip over these. You're likely to find some excellent ads — and opportunities — even in papers that publish the others.

I didn't use the smaller local presses because my (unscientific) research indicated that they not only reached fewer people, but they didn't reach the particular group of people I was aiming for. If you want to meet people in a very specific occupation, social strata, interest group or geographic location, these more tightly-targeted publications may work best.

Many publications also have separate categories and sections besides the usual Women Seeking Men/Men Seeking Women. These can include Shared Interests, Just Friends, 60+, Sports-Minded, Unmarried with Children, Travel Companion, and many others. By placing your ad under one of these categories, you can screen out people you're not interested in, while giving yourself a better chance of being seen by your best prospects.

Many larger metropolitan newspapers even have geographic lists of neighborhoods with codes for each area. When placing your ad, you can indicate either your area or the one you prefer. Using the numerical codes provided, you can avoid taking up valuable space describing where you live.

Think about the person you're trying to reach with your ad. What newspaper or magazine would they read? Create your own strategy, one that works for you and your area.

By all means consider paying to place your ad if you feel a publication reaches a significantly better audience for you. Free ads *do* work, however, and you can find the man or woman of your dreams.

I know, because I did.

VOICE MAIL TECHNOLOGY MAKES THE DIFFERENCE

It used to be that, when you placed a personal ad, the publication issued you a postal mail box number, and admirers of your ad would address letters to your mailbox in care of the publication. Generally, you paid a fee for the ad which included the postal mailbox number.

While this form of communication has some advantages — you can send and receive photographs, for example, before you decide to meet — it is a very slow way to meet people, much slower than using voice mail. And voice mail is usually free to the person who places the ad. The caller pays the fee!

Voice mail is convenient. You can get lots of voice mail, because it is easy, quick and efficient for the caller. Do you really want to meet the kind of person who has the time to write letters? Participants in letter exchange programs have been known to receive xeroxed letters. How personal is that?

I'm in favor of anything that works, and my experience is that free ads work just great. You're much more likely to receive a lot of phone calls than you are a lot of letters.

Second, it takes time for a letter to reach your mailbox at the publication, and then for it to be forwarded to your home or business. Voice mail is fast and efficient. Once your ad is published, you may be amazed at how quickly you begin to get calls — lots of calls. Most calls on an ad are made on the first day or two of publication. It is not uncommon for your ad to be published in the morning and for you to have five or more prospects to interview in the evening! Then it's just a question of who and when you want to meet.

Finally, voice mail provides a human connection that a voiceless letter cannot provide. When you listen to a message, you can often sense things that would not be obvious by reading a letter. Kindness and sincerity will shine through in a person's voice message. So will conceit and ignorance.

PRIVATE AND DISCREET

It's important to remember that, when you use personal ads, your identity is protected. Your callers can only learn your identity if and when you decide to reveal it to them.

There's a good reason for this — the publications that run the ads feel a moral obligation to protect the welfare of the participants. That's why they make sure that the responsibility to reveal your identity to a caller rests firmly with you. Many publications even go so far as to edit your message if you forget the rules and include a phone number or address in your ad or voice mail message.

The *San Diego Union-Tribune* estimates that they call back two percent of their advertisers because they make a mistake on their voice mail. The most common mistake is to include a full name or phone number. For your safety and security, this is not permitted. Also, since most publications are family oriented, they do not allow profanity or illicit suggestions. Most publications actually review the messages to ensure that these rules are followed.

Remember the guy who insisted that the newspaper pass a message on to me because he was so certain that the voice mail system was broken when I wouldn't return his calls? Despite his best efforts, the newspaper refused to give him my name, address or phone number. Although they eventually agreed to mail me his message, the confidentiality of my identity was never compromised.

THE EXECUTIVE

His voice mail message was good — he seemed sincere, successful, modest, and his voice was fabulous. This man could do radio or television commercials! When I called him back, I discovered that he had never been married, he had no children and he had an excellent education and career. He was a self-made man. After hearing all this, the only question in my mind was why he had never married. Still, the executive definitely met my criteria, and I agreed to meet him.

He chose the restaurant, which was located near my office. When I arrived, he had been watching the entrance. Clearly, my appearance met with his approval because, when I walked through the door, he bounded from his bar stool and greeted me with an outstretched hand. It felt like a scene straight out of a movie — he was the leading man, and I was his leading lady.

The Executive was a very handsome man — broad shoulders, a full head of prematurely white hair — and he was beautifully dressed. We had a wonderful evening, the first of many dates to follow. He was the last of the big-time spenders. We went to all the best restaurants. He traveled extensively, however, and sometimes had to cancel our plans at the last minute. When this happened, he always sent a fabulous flower arrangement from the most expensive florist in town.

Wow! It's hard not to be a little patient with a guy like this — even when you wonder who else he's spending time with!

Although we got along famously, the relationship eventually died a natural death. No falling out. No big scene. Our relationship just evaporated. He later called to see how I was — very classy. He then confessed that he felt I was a bit too social and outgoing for him. Although he had never mentioned it while we were dating, he preferred quiet times at home.

In any case, I was disappointed, but I was also very encouraged by the quality of men that I was meeting through the personal ads. Not long after we broke it off, The Executive married. I found this encouraging, too. A man who wanted to marry! As it turned out, his new bride had an uncanny resemblance to me!

JUMPING ON THE INFORMATION SUPERHIGHWAY

There has been a lot of recent attention directed at the wonders of the coming information superhighway. If half the claims are true, the benefits for those who jump on the bandwagon will be enormous. On-line computer services such as Prodigy, CompuServe and America Online offer services similar to the personal ads published in your local paper. There is often a fee for placing the ad for a period of time — usually two weeks or a month.

Typically, you place a descriptive ad and receive electronic mail (e-mail) messages. You can then return the e-mail with your response. If there is a common interest, you can exchange phone numbers and talk. Often, users of computer meeting services exchange photographs and addresses.

If you wish to attract the kind of person who is computer literate, this might be just the thing for you. The only downside is that you may find that your prospect lives anywhere in the country or in the world. Since most on-line services are now connected to the Internet, the worldwide network of computers, your ad can be seen by a huge audience — many of whom will be located outside your immediate vicinity. For people who travel a lot, this might not be an issue. However, if you're not interested in cultivating a long-distance romance, be absolutely sure that you specify your geographic area of interest on your Internet ad.

An older woman I know successfully used a personal ad service on the Internet. Because of her age, only a few men responded, but the ones who did were very high quality. This is because most of the computer users in her age group are well-educated and successful. As a result, she met some great men — some in the same state where she lives, others out of state.

The newest advance in using computers to place personal ads is the ability to publish personal pages on the World Wide Web — a special section of the Internet. These pages can be used to create personal profiles — complete with photographs, graphic images, personal data and even music or sound bites. Each personal page on the World Wide Web is a powerful and complete promo package. The possibilities for dating are incredible!

However, before you can create and publish your own personal page on the Internet, or even before you can place a personal ad in your local newspaper, you have to know who you are and what you want. It's all part of the process.

CHAPTER 4
Organizing for Effective Results

Finding your life-mate can be fun, but it is hard work. It's a lot of fun to listen to your messages and to call the prospects you find most interesting, but it is not nearly as much fun to get and stay organized, to remember and keep deadlines, keep up your notebook, make notes on each call and keep track of when and where you run your ads. But — and you're going to have to trust me on this one — the effort will be worth it!

I love the old adage, "The harder I work, the luckier I get!"

Your goal is to find a quality partner with whom you might be able to spend the rest of your life. If you want quality results, it is critical that you approach this task with the same kind of skill and determination you would apply to any other important business or personal project. It is particularly important to apply the skills outlined in this chapter. You are going to need a system in place to deal with the many calls you are about to receive.

It amazes me how many people try the personal ads, but quickly drop out. It takes too much effort, or they are disappointed by their initial results. This is unfortunate, because I know first-hand how well the ad process can work to achieve real happiness in life. It does take discipline and a willingness to learn and grow.

Discipline is not what you do, it's what you get. You don't give away your time or waste your energy. You effectively focus them for your benefit.

The man or woman of your dreams may call only once. If you misplace their phone number or neglect to take note of the things that most impressed you about their call, you might miss the opportunity of your lifetime.

The good news is, I have already done the hardest part for you — this book gives you a comprehensive method to help organize your personal ad process and ensure that you don't lose a single piece of information. With this system, anyone can be organized and in command of the process. The secret is planning for success by getting organized and not skipping any steps. Use this system if you really want the personal ads to work for you!

THE MOST IMPORTANT PROJECT

You don't have the time, you say? When I was running four personal ads I was a single mother of two teenagers working full-time at my real estate office while hosting a weekly cable TV series and serving on several community service boards of directors. Yet I found the time to develop and apply a very simple but organized approach to tracking my progress.

The point is, no matter how busy you are, you can always take on one more project. Especially one that will save valuable time in the long run. What could be more important than doing something for yourself? Finding the right person can enrich the rest of your life. Make it a priority.

We've all had the experience of organizing our desk at the office, or cleaning up and sorting out the garage. Isn't it a great feeling to know where everything is and be able to find it — even on short notice? It's like organizing your closet so that all your clothes are clean and ready to wear — it saves time when you're getting dressed. If you're in a hurry to get out the door, you will feel a lot more pulled together when you aren't scrambling to find the right shoes or belt or, worse yet, the button that fell off.

CHAPTER 4: ORGANIZING FOR EFFECTIVE RESULTS

The personal ads are like that, too. You will look and feel more together if you are organized. It will show in your efforts and in your results.

Let me describe exactly why you will want to be organized. Personal ads have deadlines. If you want to get your ad in a local publication, you have to submit it before the deadline. Then, before you know it, your ad expires. When your ad expires, you are out of business! When the deadline is fast approaching, you can't be scrambling around for old newspapers to find an ad form. If you are organized, you will have a file containing extra forms set aside in a drawer, where you can get your hands on it immediately, if need be, to meet your deadlines.

You will also want to keep notes on when your ads will expire. This is especially important if you are running more than one ad. Some publications run their ads for two weeks, others for four. To ensure that I always had an ad running, and that my voice mail service remained intact, I overlapped them. Instead of waiting for one ad to expire before I placed another, I would submit a variation of the original ad or, if I was fine-tuning my approach, I'd send a different ad.

Every time you run a new ad, the publication will send you a new access code for a new voice mailbox and an urgent request to place your outgoing voice message. If you aren't keeping notes and you forget the code to your new box, you won't have access to your messages. What could be worse than a voice mailbox full of personal messages that you can't access?

With the system presented in this book, you will never have to worry about that possibility.

It was great to have Beth as a partner in the ad process. We viewed the process as an adventure — who knew what kind of treasure might lie ahead for us? Sometimes, when we met at discreet locations, we felt like secret agents, or as if we were on a mini-adventure. I faxed her ad copy in to the newspaper along with mine, and we reminded each other of ad submission deadlines. Many times I had to remind her, "Have you entered your voice mail?" However, she never forgot to check her messages. Checking the messages is the fun part. But first you have to get the ad in and the voice mail on line.

Make this project a priority in your life. You will never look back and regret giving this effort your all. If you do only a half-hearted job, you can expect only half-hearted results — and the only person who loses is you.

KEEP A JOURNAL

If this sounds like homework, it is! However, keeping a journal is extremely important, and it is absolutely critical to achieving extraordinary results. It may seem like a lot of effort, but it's really just a habit. Once you get your journal or ad diary started, it's easy to keep up. Believe me, it will be worth it.

The first thing to do is to buy or create the notebook you will use for your journal. It doesn't have to be anything special — a little spiral notebook from the drugstore will do the job just fine. I suggest something small to medium in size that you can tuck away in a drawer for privacy, or carry in your purse or briefcase if you plan to check your messages or return calls while you are away from home. I used a little phony-leather calendar that someone gave me. It was a good size, so I started using it to keep notes of my phone conversations.

You will occasionally be tempted to "just this once" jot down a message on a piece of scrap paper or a Post-It® note. Avoid this temptation at all costs! If you don't make a habit of writing *all* your notes in your journal, before you know it, you will have incomplete notes. Worse still, you may lose an exciting name or phone number. I have personally proven Murphy's Law of Personal Ads many times over: You will lose names and phone numbers of prospects that are not securely recorded in your journal. Learn from my mistakes — not from your own!

There is an additional benefit in keeping your notes organized and in your journal. As you progress, and as your ads evolve, you will begin to receive messages from prospects you have already interviewed or met. By referring to your journal, you can compare names and numbers to avoid the embarrassment of calling someone you have already scratched off your list of prospects.

Once you have placed your ad, recorded your voice mail message, and established your journal — what's next? Depending on how you write your ad — how limited it is in terms of the kind of person you are looking for — you may get anywhere from just a few calls to up to 100 calls a week.

Regardless of how many calls you get, it's important to keep notes on every one. Say you get home from work and check your voice mail — you have five messages. As you are listening to the first message, write down the caller's name and phone number in your journal. Note any key information. Just jot down the important words and phrases — there is no way you are going to be able to write down the whole message, word-for-word. Here's an example:

Mark — 39, 555-1234, likes jazz, bicycling, recently divorced.

Whatever it is, make a note — as fast as you can! Voice mail works much the same as your home answering machine. You can listen to your messages over and over again in a single session, but after that, they're gone! If you write down the wrong number, it's lost — perhaps forever!

Go on feverishly taking notes on the other four messages. By the time you get to the fifth message, chances are you have already forgotten what the first caller had to say. You'll be glad you wrote it down right then instead of thinking, "Oh, I'll jot it down in a minute."

Remember Murphy's Law of Personal Ads? It has a corollary: The ad you forget to write down will be the one you want to call back (and you can't find the number!).

Get in the habit of also noting in your journal clues that might be important to your decision about whether or not to call back the person. Leave an inch or two before you go on to note your next voice mail message. This will allow space to make notes on follow-up conversations you might have later if you decide to interview your prospect.

I am a big fan of felt-tip markers. The more colors, the merrier! After I made notes on my messages, I highlighted each name and phone number with a colored marker. If the message sounded particularly interesting, I put three red stars next to it. Later, when I interviewed a prospect, I would make my notes in a different color to distinguish them from the original message.

It really doesn't matter how you separate your calls. The important thing is to be able to efficiently and accurately save the information for future reference and retrieve it when you need to. You will also want to develop a system to rate and prioritize your messages.

One more thing: Never — I repeat, *never* — throw your journal away. It is a fabulous resource. Here's an example of a time when my journal once came in handy: I had just broken up with a man I met through the personal ads, and I was without a date. Six months earlier I had received a message from a doctor living in a prestigious nearby neighborhood. Although I was interested at the time, I didn't call him back because there were other messages that attracted me more, and I became involved soon after that.

Six months later, I found myself foot-loose and fancy-free again. Knowing that it would take a couple of weeks for my new ad to appear in print, I figured, what the heck, I'll give the doctor a call! Since I had all the information recorded in my journal, it was easy for me to locate his phone number. I was a little concerned that he might be put off that it had taken me six months to return his call, so I was pleasantly surprised to find that this was not the case at all. In fact, he proceeded to tell me that he had not responded to any personal ads in quite some time, and that he had pretty much dropped out of the scene.

Coincidentally, a week before I called, he had gotten a call from another woman he had left a message with six months earlier. As a result, they had met and started dating. Although he was flattered by my call, he felt that since he and his new lady appeared to be on the verge of hitting it off, it would be inappropriate to meet me. If I had called only a week earlier, I would surely have gotten a date.

You never know when your journal might come in handy. You may even want to call to let a prospect know that you're not interested at this time, but you have a super friend who might be just right.

Your journal is an ongoing record of all the names and numbers of people who have called you. You may or may not change your ad, but your callers can and will change their voice mail messages. With your own diary, you can easily flip back and confirm names and numbers to see if they match prior voice mail names and numbers.

I recall one civil servant, a very nice man I met with once, who had an absolute, God-given talent for glorifying his job description and his position in life. Without my diary to refer to, I might have called him back many times because he always varied his messages — making them very interesting and intriguing.

I strongly believe the personal ads are not only discreet but also safe, as long as you apply normal caution and common sense in your activities. Your diary is a valuable safety net, and a sure way to establish whether calls and callers are recurring — suggesting a pattern of a potentially unstable suitor.

I never had a problem with this, and my conversations with publishers and my many friends and seminar students indicate that it is an extremely rare occurrence. Still, I prefer to be cautious, and I want you to be cautious, too. Please keep a record of all your calls!

FILE SYSTEM FOR EFFICIENCY AND FINESSE

Do you want to really impress your prospects and do an even better job of organizing your personal ad information? Keep your journal nearby to record your follow-up messages and interview conversations.

When you do choose to return a call, you often won't reach the person on the first try. In a case like this, I would make a note of the date and time that I called. I would then write a big "M" in color pen to indicate if I had left a message. That way, when I did get a return call, I could quickly find that section in my notes.

You may, for example, be returning several calls. When Sally or Bob calls you back, it's common for your mind to go blank for a moment or two. Suddenly, you can't recall if they said that they live nearby, or just arrived from Timbuktu. Reach for your diary, and you will find your notes on the caller. The same way an organized closet makes you feel better and more together, your journal will make you feel better and sound better to your caller.

First impressions do count. If you sound vague about which ad they called, or about what personal information you relayed or that they left for you, you are not going to make a good impression on your caller. You can occasionally fall back on the "gosh" technique and, in a nice way, ask your caller to help remind you of the call. However, don't rely on this technique — it's for backup use only.

If you do decide to meet for coffee, lunch, or a walk, review your notes before you meet. All of your notes on your prospect should be in one place where you can access them quickly and easily. Not only will you refresh your memory, but you can really impress your date by dropping these references into your conversation. They will be flattered when you remember the schools their children attend, or recall the fact that they were the top salesman in the region last year.

You will appear smart, poised and knowledgeable — and they will be happy that you cared enough to remember the things they consider important in their life.

HANDLING MULTIPLE ADS

If you are running more than one ad at a time, or using more than one publication, it is particularly important to establish an organized system for recording the responses you get. It can become complicated enough keeping up with the responses to just one ad — especially if it is written to attract a broad spectrum of potential callers. Multiple ads can increase your effectiveness but, at the same time, they increase the need to organize.

Running multiple ads is not necessary, but it is an option. The goal is to increase your exposure and maximize your results. The easiest way to do this is to run the same ad in more than one publication. In my area, there are two excellent publications that carry free personal ads, so I used them both. When logging my calls, I would note at the top of the page which publication they were responding to or the opening line of the ad. How awkward if, later in conversation, I referred to the wrong newspaper or the wrong ad! If someone left a message for "Golden Girl," it would be rather confusing if "Dynamic Blond Petite" called back. Not a major faux pas, but one that can be avoided.

It really starts to get complicated when you have different types of ads running in the same or different publications. If you are using more than one ad, note the opening line and the publication at the top of your journal page before you write down the voice mail messages. It only takes a second, but it really pays off later when you follow up your calls. If, as I did, you are using multiple ads for maximum exposure, you have to keep excellent records.

If running more than one ad is going to complicate matters, why bother? There are a couple of good reasons to consider giving it a try.

First, running multiple ads can maximize your results and shorten the amount of time it takes for you to meet a lasting partner. It only makes sense. If you are running one ad in a particular publication, your pool of prospects is limited to those people who read that particular newspaper or magazine. By running another ad in a second publication, you significantly increase the size of your prospect pool. Instead of getting only ten calls a week, you might get twenty or thirty. Not only will you have more people to choose from, but you will be able to be more selective in deciding whom to call back.

Publications discourage the same individual from placing more than one ad at a time. I got around this by using my own name on the ad coupons I submitted, along with my office address and phone number. I would then submit a different ad with my daughter's name and our home address and phone number.

I made it a practice to get the mail before my daughter came home, since the confirmation envelopes with voice mail instructions were so easy to recognize and claim as my own. However, it didn't take her long to catch on to my technique. I soon found this message on my desk at home: "Hi, I'm 17 yrs old & have long gingerish hair, piercingly emotional blue eyes and freckles. I am partially bilingual. I am interested in going away this weekend and, if your currency is compatible with U.S. circulation, feel free to send it to me. I can be reached at home after 2:00 P.M."

The clever brat! Her note was a little long for an ad, but it could work well for an outgoing voice mail message.

Second, running multiple ads allows you to experiment with different styles. You might run one ad, for example, that describes yourself as the "perfect executive wife." With this ad, you will definitely get responses from a certain type of prospect — most likely a successful businessman. However, if you place another ad, in the same or another publication, that describes you as a "perfect tennis partner," you will get responses from a different group. Some might be executives, but others will come from all walks of life. In any case, by running multiple ads you will be able to keep all your options open and meet and date men or women with a wide variety of backgrounds.

Finally, if you are unsure exactly what you are looking for in a partner, this is an especially effective way of helping you define key characteristics. By running ads and meeting different kinds of prospects, you can identify those characteristics you consider most important.

Experiment a little — you'll learn things about yourself, and you'll learn what words and styles appeal most to the kinds of people you want to attract. Eventually, you can make your ads more specific. Then you'll be in a better position to use your ad to attract precisely the person you seek.

Your journal will be an invaluable aid in staying on top of your different ads and keeping track of both new callers and prospects to interview. It will also help track the different kinds of people who respond to different kinds of ads.

The more ads you run, the more important it is to keep your journal up-to-date. This is especially true as you begin to screen and rate your calls.

THE JUDGE

I met The Judge because he called my girlfriend and buddy, Beth, as a result of a personal ad. Although she liked him a bit, and he had potential, she became involved with another man and decided against seeing The Judge again. Beth predicted that he would eventually call my ad — and he did. She recommended that I call him back.

I was already familiar with The Judge. He had a very highly-regarded legal career and was well known in my community. He had a vacation home in Palm Springs, along with many of the other comforts a man in the prime of his career might possess. He also had two adult children, which threw him into the top end of my desired age range — perhaps even beyond my acceptable limit. Still, I decided to take a chance and meet him for a glass of wine.

The Judge was a fine man — obviously intelligent and well-informed. However, it soon became evident that he was too old for me. It was clear that he was looking forward to retirement.

Even with careful evaluation before you meet, there will be dates that do not work out.

We had a nice enough time, but he never called me again. Maybe he could tell that I wasn't quite ready to leave everything behind and follow him into retirement.

After this meeting, I was still as optimistic as ever. If I had learned anything by now, it was to be patient. I knew that, if I kept with my program of advertising, it would not be long before I met the man I was looking for. I just knew that I was getting closer. I could feel it in my bones.

I had to keep my positive attitude intact, because the next man I spoke to just might be the one!

CHAPTER 5

Who You Are, What You Want

Do you really know who you are? Do you know what you want? Really? Your life is a journey. It started when you were still in the womb, and it won't end until you breathe your last breath. Everything you have done in your life — all the accomplishments, the mistakes, the joys and the pain — has led up to this point in your life. You are a product of your past. However, the thing that makes you uniquely human is that you have the ability to change the way you behave in the present, to create a new futures for yourself.

This chapter will show you how to discover who you are and where you want to go with the rest of your life. It can be hard to face up to your true desires. Many of us carry idealized images of these things with us. You may think, for example, that you want to find and marry a busy, successful executive, when in reality you want to meet someone who isn't a slave to long working hours, who doesn't travel much, and who will be able to dedicate lots of time to help raise a family.

In real estate, my clients often ask for one thing and end up buying something completely different. We start out looking at coastal properties and end up buying inland. Or they tell me that they absolutely *must* have a view. After months (even years!) of searching, they conclude that something else would satisfy them instead — that, in fact, they may even prefer something they had not considered before.

What you think you want and what you really want can be two very different things.

CHAPTER 5: WHO YOU ARE, WHAT YOU WANT

As you go through the exercises in this chapter, be honest with yourself. Be realistic. This is not the time to play games.

Finding the man or woman you will spend the rest of your life with is probably the most important task you will ever accomplish (not to mention one of the most rewarding)!

IDENTIFY AND DESCRIBE YOUR GOALS

Very few people know at an early age exactly what they want to be when they grow up. I was educated in the arts and worked as a volunteer and later as a professional fundraiser. Who would have thought that I would thrive as a real estate agent? Yet all the skills I learned along the way have brought a special insight and perspective to my work in finding the right home for many individuals and families. Selecting a home is like selecting a lifestyle — it suits us, nurtures us, and makes us feel comfortable.

There are no wrong answers, just many, many choices.

We all have goals. Sometimes, however, we forget what our goals are, or we submerge them to make room for someone else's goals — perhaps a boyfriend, a girlfriend, parents, kids or spouse. Trying to set goals can seem overwhelming. Like starting a diet — such a burden.

If it's been awhile since you have had clear goals — a mental picture of your life — now is the time to figure out what they are. If you don't have goals for yourself, someone else will be more than happy to include you in their goals. The trouble is, their goals may not have anything to do with where you want to be, or where you want to go with your life.

Take the time to think about what you really want from life. Without goals, you can never move forward. You will, instead, be forever destined to repeat the same old patterns over and over again.

Decide on your goals. Create a plan for your life. Write it down in your notebook. Then make sure that the ads you place, your voice mail and the people you ultimately agree to meet with all reflect those goals and fit in with your plan.

If you want to break from the past and move forward, you have to have a plan — you have to know where you are going. If you don't know where you are going, how will you know when you get there?

DREAM SEQUENCE AND REALITY CHECK

Maybe you have visions of more than one lifestyle for yourself. For years and years, I have saved, stored, stacked and moved boxes and boxes of winter clothes — just in case I move to Oregon. I live in Southern California, and it's never cold enough to wear any of those clothes. Not only that, but the chances that I'll ever move to Oregon or any other rural area are remote at best.

Yet a part of me remembers the fresh, emerald-green countryside of my childhood, and yearns for the wide-open spaces and the quiet life. Perhaps I should have run a personal ad seeking an entrepreneur who planned to leave the rat race behind and head for the hills!

What did I really want? Although I carry a romantic memory of green fields and endless horseback rides with my friends, I am no longer the little girl that I was in Michigan. I would probably be bored to death by all that quiet now. I love the excitement of the big city, the lights, the people, the arts, the theatre, the social events.

I've become a very social, gracious and talented hostess by all reports. It seemed to me that I could be a fabulous asset to a high-achieving man who wanted not only a companion, but a hostess! Surely I could manage an estate home, practice club membership, and maybe even decorate a pied-a-terre in New York...

I ended up writing an ad to attract CEOs. My ad opened with the statement "Perfect Future Corporate Wife." Needless to say, the ad attracted numerous top-level executives and company presidents — often of their own companies!

CHAPTER 5: WHO YOU ARE, WHAT YOU WANT

Some of these men were interesting, and some weren't. Slowly, with each new experience, I edited my list of preferred qualities to just the essential ones. As I reviewed my list, adding and subtracting characteristics, one item in particular became less and less important: money. Early on, I screened my candidates for significant financial resources. I was in no hurry to marry, so why not ask for everything?

As I met men of wealth, other issues came up. Some were stingy, paranoid about protecting their assets, some were spoiled by the attention they were accustomed to receiving solely on the basis of their money. Eventually, I dropped the CEO approach. I realized that, for me, a man's attitude about his work was much more important than the level of success he has achieved or how many assets he has accumulated.

I kept a list of traits I was looking for in a partner on a page of my notebook. After some trial and error, I narrowed it down to: successful, outgoing, bright, caring, honest, healthy, traditional values, affectionate and loving. This list helped me write my ads and keep focused when choosing my prospects. Today, my husband is all these things, and more.

You probably have a dream version of your destiny, too. Who hasn't dreamed of trying a new lifestyle on for size? What kind of life can you see yourself enjoying and sharing with your life partner?

Make a list of the things that you see for yourself in your new life. Maybe you have always wanted to develop a better appreciation for music. Perhaps you hope to find someone who likes to travel. Or someone who wants to start a family.

If you would like to explore the possibilities, you can write more than one ad, or change ads as your dreams and desires evolve. Don't forget — I had four different ads running for awhile.

This may seem ridiculously simple, and it is. But it helped me identify what I should be looking for in a mate. Believe me, when you have written out your list of goals, you are getting closer to *meeting* your goals.

It's a funny thing about making lists, rewriting lists, saving them and looking at them months or years later. Often, what you thought, dreamed, and wrote down on your lists comes true! Call it what you like — self-fulfilling prophecy, creative visualization, whatever. The truth is, it happens.

I tend to think that it works because you finally ask for the right thing. Writing down your dreams and visions can help you find what you really want. And, when you focus on what you really want, you will achieve it!

BE HONEST, BE YOURSELF

Now is the time to be honest with yourself. Perhaps even painfully honest. We all carry idealized images of ourselves around with us. Maybe it's an image of when you were eighteen or nineteen years old and the world was your oyster. Your mind was bright, your body was hard and your spirit was undiminished by the memory of failure or pain. Maybe it's an image of before you were married, when it seemed that every member of the opposite sex found you attractive, and you could meet people easily and freely. Maybe it's an image of a happy and successful family or career. Whatever the image is, take a cold, hard look at it, and compare it to the real you. Does it still match up?

It's time to wake up and smell the coffee. Recognize who you really are and what you really want. Above all, be yourself, and learn to be happy with that self. Sure, you aren't getting any younger, but neither is anyone else. You still have many beautiful things to share with someone special. Make a list of the things that are special about you. Your kindness, your loyalty, your athleticism, your strong beliefs, your appreciation of life, your work ethic. Write them down in your notebook and look at them often.

Forget the things that aren't really you. Many people are looking for someone just like you to share the rest of their lives with. You just have to let them know that you are out there — like a diamond in the rough — waiting to be found.

Your best prospect may be a diamond in the rough, also. Don't expect them to be perfect. Everybody has failings. Try to keep an open mind, but decide ahead of time what you can live with and what you can't. What are the deal-breakers for you? Smoking cigars? Sloppy housekeeping? A hairy back? Admit your prejudices and use them to focus your search. You may find out they're not so important after all, or they may become an essential part of the prequalifying process.

If you can't be honest with yourself, who can you be honest with? People who aren't honest with themselves aren't fooling anyone.

WORKSHEET TO GET STARTED

My neighbor Joe wrote my first ad. But Joe didn't screen my calls or interview my candidates — I had to do that. And so will you.

On a piece of paper, preferably in your notebook, begin making notes and lists. Start with the easy stuff — your age, status (single, divorced, whatever), job situation and children, if any. Sketch this information out in a brief, summary format.

Now, list your physical features — especially your best features. Your figure, eyes, smile and hair are great places to start. Everyone — men and women included — has some feature that is an asset and that stands out. What do others compliment you about? For example, people tell me that I have great hair — at any rate, it's thick and I wear it long. I also have a quick and ready smile, although I would never call it beautiful despite years of dental care.

My buddy and partner throughout the ad process, Beth, has a truly beautiful smile with pearly-white teeth that sparkle and shine every time she laughs. And, if that weren't enough, she has great, long

CHAPTER 5: WHO YOU ARE, WHAT YOU WANT

legs that have caused many a man to suffer sudden bouts of whiplash. Beth often mentioned something like "legs up to here and a gorgeous smile" in her ads. A man might say "athletic," "tall," "dark-haired," or something along those lines.

Don't make this overly complicated. Just take some time to assess and record your most attractive features. Don't just answer these questions in your head! Write them down in your notebook and refer back to them often. Change them, edit them, add to them as you discover more about yourself and the person you want to find.

Write down some words that describe your personality. You don't need to write an essay. Just put down some descriptive words. Are you shy? Outgoing? Fun-loving, intellectual, or a bookworm? If you're uncomfortable describing yourself, it might help to have a friend describe you. Or simply try to put yourself in the imaginary shoes of your greatest admirer and think how they would describe you.

I would never have described myself as "dynamic blond petite" until my friend Joe did. Then I realized that, to some people, I am dynamic blond petite.

Now, and this is easy, sketch out how you presently spend your spare time, if you have any! Do you have hobbies, favorite pastimes, a dream vacation or physical activities? How active are you? Are you very active or just barely? Jot down the answers to these questions. Your page should be filling up by now!

Living in Southern California, where people are often very health-conscious, I received voice mail messages from men who frequently mentioned that they worked out daily or had a big commitment to jogging, golf or tennis. These are very positive habits, and not ones I am incompatible with. But, since I'm casual about my exercise, I felt that someone with a high standard of fitness might find me a bit unfit. Beth adores tennis and golf, and occasionally included that fact in her voice mail, while I pretty much steered clear of references to my physical activities, and instead mentioned art and museums.

Okay, now it's time to write down even more positive words about you. Are you successful? Energetic? Devoted? Caring? A great cook? Write down every word you can think of. We may not use all these words, but they will help you get to know who you are and all that you bring to a relationship.

Finally, write down what you are seeking in a mate in approximately the same sequence as the information about yourself. Jot down age, occupation, marital status, children, and educational level if that is a priority for you. At this point, you don't have to be precise. Your answers may be a range — for example, you might consider the age range of 35 - 45 to be of interest to you. Consider what kind of career your intended mate is likely to have. You may make the wrong choices initially, but at least this process poses the question of what kind of mate will likely suit you. The answers might include: school teacher, architect or entrepreneur — for many of us, there is more than one answer. The success level you desire may range from very successful to just employed. In answer to children, you might consider no children, teenagers okay, or a desire to start and raise a family.

Continue with activity levels, athletic interests and appearance. Maybe looks are an important aspect for you. Maybe not. What kind of personality would complement yours? Quiet? Outgoing? Social? Beliefs or religion may be important issues for you. If so, be sure to write them down.

Making these lists can be an exercise in self-discovery. You may learn things about yourself, and about your needs and desires, that you were unwilling to admit or unable to recognize before. Don't be afraid. Don't be judgmental, and don't say what you think you ought to say. Be real. This is one place where candor can't hurt you.

You're going to find someone who wants the same things you do, who is looking for just the kind of person you are. You'll know that they're interested in you — the real you — because they responded to your ad.

WORDS THAT WORK

Here is a very powerful list of words you can use to describe who you are and who you are looking for. This list is by no means all-inclusive. Add to this list, or create your own. Ask your friends for their input. Above all, have fun!

Words that work will be words that describe you and who you seek in a positive way that others can relate to and be drawn to. Many of the words have connotations that are common to all of us. However, each one of us has our own vision of what a word means. Take the word "successful," for example. Some people see success solely in terms of money, some as business status or social position. Fortunately, if the wrong person calls, you don't have to call back.

"Attractive" is another word that means different things to different people. What exactly is attractive? Or "beautiful"? Beauty is in the eye of the beholder. By all means, use these words if they are appropriate for you and who you are seeking.

Blond petite	Country girl
Dynamic brunette	Slender not!
Energetic girl next door	Upscale
Exotic intellectual	Complete package
Successful career gal	Smart
Career-minded	In shape
Marriage-minded	Great legs
Conservative	Lighthearted
Educated	Compatible
Romantic	Discriminating
Athletic	Secure

CHAPTER 5: WHO YOU ARE, WHAT YOU WANT

Attractive	Dancing fool
Exciting	Unencumbered
Pretty	Former debutante
Passionate	Nice
Goal-oriented	Foxy
Sophisticated	Artistic
Articulate	Go-getter
Outgoing	County-loving
Funny	Graceful
Elegant	Cuddly
Traffic-stopping	Young
Statuesque	Mellow
Head-turner	Middle-aged
Fabulous	Fearless
Charming	Playful
Witty	Passionate
Lovely	Straightforward
Compassionate	Dreamer
Caring	Fun
Brilliant	Romantic
Happy	Grounded
Stunning	Sincere
Holistic	Classy
Beautiful	Old-fashioned
Affectionate	Responsible
Spirited	Good-hearted
Spiritual	Literary
Eccentric	Politically progressive
High-spirited	Creative
Sports fan	Hispana matrimoniales
Queen size	Scandinavian American

CHAPTER 5: WHO YOU ARE, WHAT YOU WANT

Kissable	Canadian
Voluptuous	Latin
Unconventional	British
Professional	Asian
Cultured	Silver fox
Thin	Relationship
Slender	Romantic
Dark-eyed	Monogamous
Well-built	Love & romance
Fiery redhead	Serious relationship
Pixie	Adventure, travel & bliss
Fair-haired	Tennis, music & travel
Cute	Sense of humor & curves
Freckles	Live your dream
Physically fit	Physically and financially fit
Shapely	Savor life with the perfect person
Olive-skinned	Serious only need apply
European	Life's variety and simplicity
Ebony	Lasting partnership
Runner	Long-term love
Tanned	Movies, music & dancing
Hourglass figure	Mellow lady & more
Well-endowed	Like-minded
Looker	Life-mate
Muscular	Mutually rewarding
Lean	Possible long-term
Compact	Explore life
Clean-cut	Prince Charming
Positive	Partner in crime
Humorous	Spiritual quest
Naughty but nice	Simple pleasures

CHAPTER 5: WHO YOU ARE, WHAT YOU WANT

Super nice	Meaningful companionship
Uncomplicated	Future together
Ambitious	Friends first
Lonely	Marriage possible
Non-jock	Honesty, love, care and friendship
Praying	Spend life together
Engineer	Intimate times
MBA	Fun and mutual happiness
Secure	Children OK
Liberal	Likes children
Open minded	Smoker
Quality	Non-smoker
Homespun	Golfer
Fabulous job	North Coastal
Patient	South Bay
Easygoing	Financial freedom
Perfect wife	Yogi Bear

This list of words will help get you started, but you may find other words that fit you or your personality better. If so, use them! This list is simply a place for you to start — the words have been carefully selected from many real personal ads, and have been very successful for their users.

One last note. I find it very interesting that often the men's and women's ads are really quite similar in what they are seeking. Although I don't encourage calling on other people's ads (because I feel it's an unnecessary expense and you're not in control of the situation), you can benefit by reading them.

Take the time to regularly review other ads and note any particularly interesting words that you can use in your own. If you're really intrigued by an ad, don't be afraid to call!

WHAT WILL NOT WORK FOR YOU

Sometimes it's hard to know what will not work for you until you give it a try. Placing personal ads can be very much a trial-and-error process. Keep records of all your ads in your notebook. Write the text of the ad down, or tape the newspaper or magazine clipping into your notebook, along with the responses your ad received, making additional notes regarding the nature of the callers.

For example, if your ad only gets five responses — none of whom meet your criteria — make a note of that and try a new set of words. If you get a better response with the new ad, then use that information, and fine-tune your ad to make it even better.

One thing that definitely *won't* work is fooling yourself and your callers with words that don't really describe who you are or who you want to be.

Be honest with yourself, and straightforward with your candidates. If your idea of heaven on earth is sitting in front of the television, say so. If you loathe TV or are an opera groupie, it would be prudent to mention that in your ad or voice mail message. Whatever your issues are, be as candid as possible.

By all means, have your dreams. Then do a reality check on who you are and what kind of person you are truly going to attract. This may sound contradictory, but it's not. The best way to have wonderful things happen to you is to be wonderful. You can do it!

Writing personal ads is a process. You can change your ad easily, and you can let your ad evolve as time goes on. You may find that your perspective and your goals evolve also, while you open yourself to possibilities never considered before.

In real estate, we evaluate the future potential of a piece of land by asking "What is the highest and best use?" What is your highest and best use? What kind of person are you today and what kind of person do you aspire to be tomorrow?

Being honest isn't the same as being negative. Don't be afraid to dream. Be the best you can be. Concentrate on your highest and best use — on the things that will work for you.

THE CHIEF EXECUTIVE OFFICER

The Chief Executive Officer left several messages on my voice mail but I had not returned any of them. I'm not sure why I hadn't. My advertisement said I would be the "perfect future corporate wife." And here was the perfect CEO. Maybe it was because the message he left on my voice mail was a little too slick — too well-rehearsed — even a bit pompous and pretentious. When I heard it again in response to another one of my ads, his message sounded much the same. Finally curiosity — or boredom — led me to return his call.

The CEO seemed pleasant enough. Our phone interview went well. Nothing was said to discourage me from meeting him. It turned out that he was the founder and president of a firm with offices in Washington D.C. and San Diego, California. He had older children, and was apparently very active. He was at the high end of my age range, but I decided to take a chance. Why not? Age is relative, after all.

We met at the bar of a very nice hotel near my home. He was very pleased to meet me, but it didn't take me long to realize that the CEO was just too old. Despite his success, I felt as if we were from different generations, that we didn't have anything in common. Although he was interested, I wasn't. There just wasn't any spark for me. I knew I would have to keep looking.

CHAPTER 6

Create Your Own Ad

You have had some time by now to think about your own ad. You may have already jotted down a few ideas. If so, that's great! If you haven't, don't worry — in this chapter, you're going to learn how to design and create an ad that is perfect for you.

The whole process of using the personal ads to find a mate can and should be exciting and a lot of fun. It's really not that complicated. Your first ad will often be your best ad. But don't forget that part of the fun of using the personal ads is that you can change your ad any time you want. Don't overburden yourself — just do it!

It's important to create a personal ad that gets the attention of the reader and that highlights your best attributes. Take a look at the personal ads in your local newspaper to see how other people use them to describe themselves — and who they hope to meet. Save these sections, because they will include the instructions for submitting your ad.

One of the first things you will notice is that personal ads are just that — personal. This is your chance to put your best foot forward.

OPENING LINES TO GET ATTENTION

Almost every ad has two distinct parts. These parts are interchangeable and they sometimes overlap. The first part of the ad describes you — it could include your gender, your hair color, your great legs, your age, your marital status, your dashing smile, and many other things. For example:

CHAPTER 6: CREATE YOUR OWN AD

PETITE, SENSUOUS, 5', 104 lbs., 51, fun-loving, attractive, open, honest, monogamous...

The second part of the ad describes the person you are seeking. This is where you might specify the age range of your prospects, their interests, physical attributes, their attitude toward things you feel are important and other such considerations. The ad above continues:

...Seeking secure, unencumbered, attractive, white, 48-54, 5'8"+, romantic, attentive, trim, healthy, humorous, varied interests.

If you leave this out, you will lose one of the big advantages of using the personal ads: The ability to weed out those who don't suit you before you spend any time on them. You'll get such diverse calls that it will take forever to weed through them all.

It sounds like fun to get dozens and dozens of calls, but you could wear yourself out listening to that many and miss the one good one.

Occasionally, an ad will only describe the person being sought — often in very flowery verse. The general rule, however, is to start by describing yourself, and then describe who it is you are seeking.

The opening line is the key to your personal ad. Virtually every publication prints the first few words in some sort of distinctive typeface. Some publications use bold type, others use all capital letters. The idea is to catch the eye of the reader — and, indeed, many readers will just scan these opening lines when they are in a rush and are reading through a lot of ads.

It is to your advantage to have a good opening line. What's yours? Is it "Tall Brunette?" Or "Athletic Tennis Player?" Whatever it is, be honest — but this is also your opportunity to embellish or even exaggerate a little.

MEET YOUR DREAM GIRL. Very attractive, long hair,

brown eyes, fit, 135 lbs., 5'5", 30s (looking younger), pretty smile, great personality, outgoing, loving, sincere. Enjoy the beach, theater, movies, arts, travel, coffee shops, more. Seeking romantic professional, creative, white, tall, stable, sense of humor, honest gentleman for meaningful relationship.

An attention-getting opening line is a great tool — try for a strong or catchy beginning. Remember, this is advertising. Put some zip into an opening that works for you!

CASTING NOW for romantic comedy. Play opposite tall, slender, feisty, gorgeous redhead. Scenes include action, romance, adventure. Cast calls for tall, gorgeous man with great sense of humor, can easily ad lib, ages 35-45.

Some ads are so creative they are confusing. For example, this one is from a San Diego newspaper:

WILD SHOE COLLECTION: stilettoed thigh-high boots, five-inch pumps & dainty mules seeks polished, well cared for wingtips for long-term admiration & fun.

This is very cute, but if the author is truly seeking long-term admiration, she is going to have to wade through all kinds of offbeat messages. I hope she has some wading boots in her collection, too!

This ad makes no mention of age group or other parameters, but it is attention-getting, so she will probably get a lot of calls. But what kind of calls? Maybe she could set up a string of interviews — have them line up and give them each five minutes.

Is the purpose of your ad to be cute and get random, off-the-wall calls? Or is it to effectively seek a specific result?

If your goal is to meet a lot of people — any kind of people of any age — then a fun ad like the following will suit your purposes. However, you can get much better results with a fairly straightforward, specific approach.

> **ROSES ARE RED, my eyes are blue, if you're good-natured, and fun-loving too, perhaps a rendezvous? Attractive professional, 42, 5'10", active, artistic, caring.**

I question the effectiveness of ads that are overly humorous or thematic unless this is a strong part of your personality, and reflects an attribute that you hope to attract.

A candid, truthful approach with a touch of flair works best. You can't go wrong, and you will get the results you seek.

DESCRIPTIVE WORDS TO MARKET AND TARGET

Descriptive words are just that — words that describe who you are and the kind of person you want to meet. There is often more than one way to say the same thing. Which sounds better to you? "Dynamic Blond Petite," or "Small, Energetic Blond?"

How about the opening lines my friend Beth used? Which do you like better? "Gorgeous Smile and Legs Up to Here" or "Great Smile and Long Legs?"

There are no right or wrong answers to these questions. Some people will respond more favorably to one than the other. They both say the same thing, just in different ways.

Don't forget, you're not creating the ad to please yourself as much as you are to attract callers. When you create your ad, think about the person you want to respond to it. What will be better for them?

Select words that will attract the audience you are seeking. Depending on who you wish to attract, plain words may be best. If you are looking for a sophisticated member of the opposite sex, you may find that they respond better to a larger vocabulary.

EXISTENTIALLY PENSIVE, intelligent, adventurous, emotionally lively woman, 46, seeks idea-loving, kind man. Vive Buber, Bettelheim, Grafton, jazz, Chagall. You?

I have noticed the term "esoteric tastes" in several ads. Using phrases like this tells quite a bit about you. First, it assumes that the user knows what "esoteric" means and, second, it says you are looking for someone a little out of the ordinary. "Celestial," "eclectic," "advocate" — these words also indicate a certain level of sophistication. Sometimes an obscure or off-center word or phrase is a great way to encourage a quality response.

References to opera, education or a professional career clearly indicate a higher level of sophistication both offered and sought.

STUNNING IN BLACK VELVET, playful in jeans. We're tall, professional, cultured, centered. Enjoy opera, travel, beach, intimacy. 52 & soaring.

Your choice of words has a major effect on the responses you receive. Remember the word "dynamic" that I used in the opening line of my ad? One man told me that he was intimidated by my use of that particular word. He confessed that, when he called my voice mailbox for the first time, he didn't have the nerve to leave a message. But he liked what my voice mail said, and later decided to call back and leave a message. We became good friends as a result, but I have to confess that he was a timid man. It all adds up!

Step into the shoes of your prospects, and view your ad from their perspective. What will attract them? What will put them off? What do they expect to hear? What do they expect to learn?

Each word you choose carries its actual, dictionary meaning, plus the connotations it brings to mind. You can never tell for sure how a reader will interpret the words you use in your ad, and it may take a few tries before you get it right.

Eventually, you will sharpen your ad into a finely-honed advertisement of yourself, geared toward the person you want to spend the rest of your life with.

Your goal is to select the best words that create the most positive image of you to attract the attention of quality prospects.

SPECIFICS TO DIRECT AND NARROW RESPONSE

What do you think of this ad?

YOUNG PROFESSIONAL, enjoys travel, romantic sunsets, beach, runs/walks, working out together, movies. Ages 24-34. Shall we also share Paris this spring?

This ad does a beautiful job of creating a mental image of the person that the user is seeking. Not only that, but it uses very specific words and information to narrow the responses to those who meet certain criteria — a love of fragrant cafe au lait and savory French pastries from a small Parisian boulangerie around the corner from an intimate hotel room apparently being foremost on the list! In this case, the ad was placed by a man seeking a woman, but it could just as easily have been placed by a woman seeking a man. This ad also shows that you don't have to make the ad writing more complicated than it need be. The ad is simple, straightforward and direct. The closing line has a lot of charm, and it enhances the ad.

Don't be intimidated by having to select just twenty or twenty-five words for your free ad. Just sketch it out and send it in! Once you have placed your ad, keep trying different versions, substituting words until you have a combination that works best for you.

Your goal is to describe yourself in such a way that the reader can

CHAPTER 6: CREATE YOUR OWN AD

make an informed decision in selecting your ad and deciding whether or not it applies to them. Help your prospects find you by choosing words that tell them who you really are.

If you don't get a great response right off the bat, don't worry. There's nothing wrong with you. There's just something wrong with your ad — and that's easy to fix. Don't give up!

Here's an ad that once caught my eye.

POLO PLAYER, IVY League graduate and international businessman, age 48, seeks attractive woman ages 35-45 for poetry and more.

I liked that ad so much, in fact, that I called his voice mail. I had just broken up with a gentleman I met through the personal ads, and I hadn't yet found the time to get an ad back in the paper. I was ready, however, to get out and meet some new men.

When I read the ad, all kinds of images came to my mind — I was curious to meet this man. I paid the small fee to leave a message on his voice mail, and I left my name and phone number so he could call me back. Naturally, I used the same skills in leaving my message as I used in creating an outgoing voice message for my own personal ads.

He promptly returned my call. He told me that he returned very few messages, but that he was very interested in meeting me. He commented that my voice mail message to his ad was better than the others that he received. Since my message was interesting and detailed, it made him want to call back promptly.

We went out a number of times and, although his ad puffed up his image a bit, it was basically correct. Through the judicious selection of words, The Polo Player had attracted me — I was just the kind of woman he was looking for. If one or two of the words had been different, I might never have called to begin with.

Here's another example.

LOVE IS UNCONDITIONAL. Secure romantic, 6'5", mid-50s, desires woman, trim, healthy, energetic, assertive or career-minded for long-term relationship.

What kind of man do you think placed this ad? This sounds like someone who is ready to settle down and who has given some serious thought to what would work for him. Once again, the ad provides very specific information to help narrow the responses to those who meet specific criteria. He is clearly looking for an assertive woman, the type who might have a career, although he was nice enough to let us know that the career is not essential. He would be happy with just assertive.

I like this guy already! He doesn't object to a woman who has her own opinions — he welcomes it. And he went to the trouble of telling us his age and height. This is all useful information for a prospect, enough to help you easily make a decision on whether to respond to the ad.

Tell them what you want, and it is much more likely that you will get it! Here's one last example of the use of specific words to direct and narrow the responses.

WIFE WANTED Happy Valentine's Day every day, white male, 56/5'8"/180 seeking sincere, loving, marriage-minded lady. 20-40s, no smoke/drugs/drink.

It doesn't get much more direct than this! Why waste time? My only criticism of the ad is the wide age range that the user has indicated. What does this fifty-six-year-old man have to offer to a woman in her twenties, unless marriage is her only goal?

At least he is being honest about who he is hoping to meet. Clearly, any woman who is seeking a marriage-minded man will give this ad a close look.

THE ITALIAN STALLION

The voice of the message he left on my voice mail had an East Coast accent — the type that to me means humble origins. However, beyond the initial impression of his accent, the tone and content of his message was pretty exciting — a retired naval officer involved in several different entrepreneurial pursuits. This man was active and energetic, and his age was just a few years above mine.

From his phone prefix, I knew that he lived in the same area as I did — a very desirable, upscale coastal area. When I returned his call, it just got better. Never married, no children, home owner. He sounded energetic, and he was clearly still excited about his life. When he mentioned the neighborhood he lived in, my respect for his good choice only confirmed that he was a bright man — a man I would like to meet.

We agreed to meet for brunch that weekend. Our conversation was lively. He was financially solvent, but willing to take risks and make investments in his own projects. He also turned out to be very fit and attractive. His style was a bit more colorful than mine, but there were a lot of things that I liked about him. We agreed to go out to dinner.

He picked me up and suggested that we go to his place for a glass of wine, since our dinner reservations were for later. His home was lovely — stunning views and beautifully decorated. The most unusual aspect of his home was the mirrors. There were mirrors everywhere! While they were elegant in the living room, they were quite overwhelming in his bedroom. Fascinating!

Although we had a fun dinner, I never went back to his home. And, although we indicated we would get together again, we never did. The Italian Stallion was certainly not dull or boring. He was a little too flashy for me, but great fun to meet!

Despite the fact that this prospect didn't pan out, I was still encouraged. I had met yet another handsome, successful, active man. I knew I was on the right track. I was meeting high-caliber, interesting men who were both eligible and available. I was convinced that they were out there, and that they were looking for a nice girl like me.

It was just a matter of time before I found the man I would spend the rest of my life with. Until then, I would keep advertising, keep meeting quality men, and have a lot of fun in the process!

WRITING YOUR AD

Okay, it's time to draft your ad. You have twenty, maybe twenty-five words at most to get your message across to your prospects.

Your ad has to be many things. It has to be catchy, it has to tell the reader something about you, and something about who you are seeking. Finally, your ad has to make your reader call your voice mailbox for more information.

Set up a worksheet with the following headings:

Opening Line or Phrase

Self Description

Description of Person You're Seeking

Save copies of the personal ad section of the publications you plan to use. The format will vary. We will assume that you are limited to twenty-five words — you can always expand with words from your list if space permits.

Start with the opening line — this is the part of your ad that will be boldfaced or in capital letters. Many readers glance over the opening lines, pausing to read the ones they are first attracted to.

Before you start putting down ideas for your opening line, look for a positive, catchy slant on who you are. For help, review the word lists in Chapter Four. Sometimes a single word is all that's required.

ADORABLE! Long hair, blue eyes, great smile, playful, Class A, 40. Please be warm, outgoing, educated, confident, with boyish good looks. Humor a must!

If you need more ideas, look over the personal ads in your local paper, or ask a friend to help describe you. The words you choose should accurately describe who you are, but with a hook that makes the reader want to learn more about you.

Go ahead, fill in the opening line portion of your worksheet. Maybe you are an Energetic Girl Next Door. Or an Articulate Dancing Fool. Or a Perfect Wife. Whatever you are, write it down.

Next, give the reader more details about yourself. Your age, sex, interests, likes and dislikes. If you like romantic candlelight dinners and hate TV dinners, this is the place to let the world know! Maybe you like kids and you hope to have a family, or maybe you love to travel and are looking for someone to join you on a cruise to the Caribbean.

This part of your ad should take approximately ten words — depending on how many words you decide to devote to the rest of the ad.

ATTRACTIVE, DEGREED professional, 48, 5'9-3/4", auburn/blue. Enjoys outdoors, theater, movies, dancing...

This is just a sketch. Rewrite and fine-tune it before you actually submit it for publication. You may find that you are having a hard time fitting everything into only ten words. That's okay. You will be able to give your prospects a much more detailed description of yourself in your voice mail message.

You want to condense your description down to the most important details — the ones that will help create a picture of you in your reader's mind, and make him pick up the telephone to learn more about you.

CHAPTER 6: CREATE YOUR OWN AD

Next, write a description of the person you are seeking. Take another look at the word lists. If you are seeking a "physically and financially fit partner in crime for fun and mutual happiness," then by all means write it down on your worksheet in the space provided for the description of your ideal prospect.

...Looking for peaceful, easygoing relationship with intelligent, down to earth white male who is mechanically inclined, independent, non-smoker.

I have said it before, and I will say it again — tell them what you want! Don't worry about scaring away prospects by saying those dreaded "C" words. You know, "commitment," "caring" and "communication." If something is important to you, it is infinitely better to get it on the table now, before you have established a relationship, than after you have invested months or even years in it.

...wants easygoing, tender, honest, lives in the "now," no baggage, monogamous, open, committed man.

Be careful what you ask for — you might get it! Be honest, be true to yourself, and you won't have any problems at all.

Now, take a look at the ad you have drafted. Does it have all the parts? You should have a short opening line, a description of yourself, and a description of the person you are hoping to meet.

Once you are happy with the words you have used and the way you have used them, you're done!

Finally, you might show a copy of your ad to a close friend — someone who knows you well and isn't afraid to give you a little constructive criticism. Your friend might point out an important personal attribute that you left out, or they may help you fine-tune your message or redirect it to the audience you really desire.

Here is a summary of the key points to cover in your personal ad:

1. Five words about you: age, physical, and personal details.
2. Up to ten more words about your best traits or features, and hobbies.
3. Up to ten words about the person you would like to meet: age, traits, lifestyle, and what kind of relationship you are seeking.

You're done. It's that simple!

EXPERIMENTING WITH DIFFERENT APPROACHES

This is the fun part. After you place your first ad, take careful note of the responses you receive. What kind of responses are you getting? Are you attracting the kind of people that you hoped for? If so, fantastic! You might want to stick with that ad until you find your life mate. However, if you aren't getting much of a response, or if the responses you are getting seem to be off base, you should experiment with some new ads and voice mail messages.

At this point, you should be using your notebook to keep track of everything you do related to the personal ad process. There is just no way you can remember every ad you place, and the name, phone number, and description of every caller who responds to your ads. Your notebook makes this process much more organized and much more manageable. It remembers everything for you. When you get a call, make notes about the caller in your notebook. Then, if you decide to call back, you'll be able to quickly and easily find your notes, go over them and be able to relate details about yourself that match the information provided to you.

Use your notebook to keep track of what ads work best for you, even the particular words that seem to attract your best prospects. Since you aren't paying for the ad, there is no penalty to you when you change it. You are free to change it as often as you want until it is as finely tuned as it can possibly be. Every time you change your ad, make a note of the change in your notebook, or just tape a copy of your ad onto one of your notebook pages. Your journal of calls will indicate how much response each ad approach is getting. If you're having great success, stay with that approach. If you continue to submit it for publication, vary it just a little to keep it fresh. If your success is still around the corner, try a new approach!

If at first you don't succeed — well, you know the rest! Experiment with different approaches until you find the one that works best for you. But keep trying. Sometimes a slow or reduced response simply represents a lull in the process. Maybe it's a busy time of year, maybe personal problems or work pressures are keeping your prospects from calling. Response will vary for any number of reasons. Don't assume it's your fault.

If you are really organized, you can run several ads at the same time just to see which one attracts the best candidates for you. If you are uncertain about the kind of person you are seeking, this is an especially good technique to employ to help you define your objectives. In my area, there was more than one excellent free ad publication, so I could try a different approach in each. You may need to use different addresses if you run more than one ad in the same publication, however.

When you start experimenting with different ads, it becomes even more important to employ an organized approach to using the personal ads. Organization is vital to the ultimate success of your search. It's the only way to stay in command of the process.

PLACING YOUR AD

Most publications require you to fill out a special form to place your personal ad. The form will typically be found in the personal ad section of the publication, and it will ask you to provide your name, address, phone number, and your ad copy. Your name, address, and phone number will remain confidential — only your ad will be printed.

CHAPTER 6: CREATE YOUR OWN AD

You will probably have the option of mailing in your ad or faxing it to the publication. If you can fax, it will be received much more quickly than if you mail it in. This may be an important consideration if you are approaching the ad deadline.

Unless you place your ad in one of the specialized publications that requires a fee, your ad will be free, and you need not worry about enclosing a fee with it. The people who call your voice mailbox pay for the privilege of listening to your message. After your ad is received and processed, you will be issued a voice mailbox phone number and a secret code. Only you will have the secret code and only you will have access to the voice mailbox.

As soon as you receive your voice mailbox number and your secret code, you will want to record your voice mail message. You may only have a short period of time from the issuance of a voice mailbox and the publication of your ad. If that someone special calls in response to your ad and there is no message to listen to, you can bet that he won't call back!

Your voice mail message goes beyond the limitations of your printed ad and tells the listener more about you. Voice mail is the heart of the modern personal ad process. If you can master it, you will be successful beyond your wildest dreams!

CHAPTER 7

Voice Mail: The Real You

Electronic message transferring systems have truly transformed and revolutionized communications worldwide. Cable TV on phone lines, computer services on cable TV lines — it continues to change, and it is multifaceted.

Telecommunications have also revolutionized the dating game and social rituals. Two aspects that specifically relate to the personal ads and finding your perfect life mate are: (1) your exposure is vast (and fast), and (2) you communicate before you meet. We now have an expansive marketplace of single people, and we have efficient, easy, and convenient access to each other.

These changes have altered dating patterns and traditional techniques of meeting and getting to know someone. I call this the New Etiquette. You ask personal questions in advance and get information that normally is not available until much later in a relationship.

With voice mail, you can record a very detailed description of yourself and the kind of person you are looking for, one that goes far beyond the brief ad you placed in the newspaper. While your printed ad serves as an initial way to attract and screen prospects, your voice mail message helps you target your audience and screen your prospects much more precisely.

Since callers can leave a response immediately, you are able to make a connection with them as soon as you play back your messages and decide who you want to find out more about. No waiting for them to write you a letter. No waiting for the mail carrier to arrive.

You can literally receive a call at 11:00 A.M., listen to it a few minutes later, call back and make a date for lunch that very same day. It's that quick — and it's that simple.

It's important to construct a voice mail message that will work efficiently and effectively for you. This message is a fabulous opportunity to tell your prospects more about yourself, and more about the kind of person you are hoping to meet. Take the time to make it shine!

The following voice mail message is a good example of putting your best foot foward. It was connected with an ad that started "Future Corporate Bride."

> **Thank you for calling Future Corporate Bride! That may sound pretentious... but perhaps you've heard the expression, "highest and best use." You may not need a corporate wife, but I'm very attracted to the concept because I believe I would excel in a supportive commitment to a man I respect. I'm attractive, of course. 5-foot-6, 110 lbs., fit, wonderful legs, intelligent face that is also quite pretty. My talents are very broad. I'm gracious, adept at all social levels and a natural facilitator in any group or event. I'm really overqualified for this position, but I would enjoy it. I have a lot of love to give. It's really my only disappointment in life, because I have everything else. Leave me a message if you think it's appropriate, and I'll try to get back to you.**

IT'S TIME TO GET REAL

One of the women who attended my seminar had called in response to personal ads before, but she had never placed her own ad. My seminar inspired her to place her first personal ad. As a result, she received quite a few messages, but one in particular caught her attention. It's a good example of how voice mail influences this process.

The caller on her voice mail sounded very nervous, but my client felt a ring of truthfulness in his voice. She didn't want to meet someone who was too polished. In his message, he mentioned that he had tried numerous dating services and singles groups, but he had not yet found the kind of person he was seeking — a woman with compassion. Something about his use of the word "compassion" touched her heartstrings. This was a man she wanted to meet.

And meet they did. Today, they are a devoted couple, and they plan to marry. Both agree that, without the personal ads, they might never have found each other.

The key to using voice mail is to be real — be yourself. Although the man in the above example was nervous about leaving a message, he opened up his heart to my client. He bared his soul to her and, in the process, allowed my client to see him for what he really was — a man with feelings and heart. A man she might want to meet. If he had put on a false front, if he had disguised his nervousness with cocky bravado, or if he had tried to bowl her over with his wit or force of personality, she wouldn't have given his message a second thought. And they never would have met.

If you pretend to be someone you're not, how can you find the right someone for who you really are?

TOOLS FOR TARGETING YOUR AUDIENCE

One basic tool you use for targeting your audience is to describe yourself. Another tool is to describe who it is that you are seeking. Generally, you will do both when you place a personal ad. In fact, the combination of your printed ad and your voice mail message gives you ample opportunity to do both. Voice mail works to amplify the information in your ad and balance your caller's initial impression with more information.

Think of your ad and your voice mail message as a team, working together symbiotically to paint a picture of the real you. The more information you convey, the more easily your prospects can screen themselves before they respond to your ad.

I had a lot of luck with the ads I ran that began with "Golden Girl." I thought this was a pretty catchy beginning and, indeed, so did the many men who responded to it. Then I used my outgoing voice mail message to qualify, target, and screen prospects. Typically, I began my voice mail message by repeating my opening line.

> **Thank you for calling Golden Girl. I do sort of feel like a golden girl. I've had many blessings in life, and most of the benefits. Of course, the fact that I work hard may have something to do with it. And I confess I do have a wonderful lifestyle and golden hair! I own a charming home practically on the beach here in North County and, frankly, I hope you own your own home also. My education is in the arts. Although it's no longer my career, it remains my avocation and I'm very involved in the visual arts community, primarily as an advocate and fundraiser. It's been a significant part of my life, and I have the opportunity to give something back. I'm very healthy, in all ways. I exercise and keep fit. I'm petite, 5'6", 110 lbs., and I have long legs — great legs according to some. Anyway, life is short, but very wonderful. My work and volunteer projects keep me very busy, so if it is your desire that I return your call, please leave me some personal information that would encourage me to! Best wishes from the Golden Girl.**

I had a very good response to this combination of ad with a catchy opening line, plus a voice mail message that told the caller more about me. Certainly, not everyone wants to meet a former artist who is so heavily involved in her community, so I made a point of letting them know my situation in advance, and letting them decide if I was the right woman for them. I also made a point of encouraging my prospects to leave some substantial personal information for me to consider.

Did you also notice the "buzz" words in the ad? "Avocation" is one. A smart caller will draw some information about me from that word. My message also made the point that I'm looking for someone who owns their own home. Since I mentioned that I own my home, they should understand that it's not because I need a new home. The simple fact is, someone in my age group who doesn't own their own home probably has some extenuating circumstances that would remove them from my list of eligibles anyway.

If they left a message that said something to the effect, "I don't presently own my own home because I am new to the area," or "I recently sold my home in La Jolla, and I am currently in the market for a new one," I would understand. Not owning a home is not necessarily a deal breaker in my mind — it's just a good way to start the screening process.

MIRROR EFFECT — TELL THEM ABOUT YOU

More often than not, a person responding to your ad will give you much the same information that you share with them. This is a very natural reflex, and it can be very helpful in getting an initial impression of your caller. I ran the following ad, giving a lot of information about myself in just a few words:

PRIME TIME! Age 43 petite blond with great legs! Thin, fit, successful, passionate & caring, N. Coast homeowner seeks accomplished gentleman age 43-50.

CHAPTER 7: VOICE MAIL — THE REAL YOU

The voice mail message I used in conjunction with this particular ad followed up the physical information I gave in the ad with more personal information about my feelings and attitudes:

Thank you for calling Prime Time. I do feel this is the prime of my life. I'm a little chagrined to be participating in this process — however, maybe it's a perfect solution for the busy lives we lead. My clients and friends are invariably amazed that I don't have more male suitors, but I work long hours and I don't seem to meet eligible men interested in a traditional relationship...

Guess you would like some facts. I am 43, 5-foot-six, 115 pounds, blond and intelligent. I own my own home, practically on the sand, and I hope you do, too. I'm health oriented, but not a fanatic! Mostly I bike along the beach colony, walk, swim, just keep busy!

I'm looking for a man who has a twinkle in his eye that indicates something going on in there — hopefully a sense of humor and an interest in life. If you're successful and happy with your life, I'd like to know more about you. Do leave me a message and indicate the best time to contact you. Best wishes from Prime Time.

The response to a message like the one above is likely to be similar, speaking as much about feelings as about facts. Providing a deeper insight to yourself is a good way to generate a lot of in-depth information from your caller.

The responses you get won't always be as forthcoming as you'd like, however. Sometimes you will receive a message that sounds either too smooth, too rehearsed or too pompous. It's not rare for a caller to have a scripted synopsis about themselves that they wish to leave with you, no matter what your message asks for. Trust your first impression. If something doesn't sound quite right with the caller or the message, jot down the name and number and go on to the next.

I have received messages that immediately turned me off and made me feel quite certain that I did not care to meet the caller. I have also received extremely brief messages that gave me little information, and therefore no reason or encouragement to call back. These messages were added to my journal of calls, but were given a low priority for calling back. Since I always had plenty of calls to consider, and it was impossible to return them all, I first called the people who attracted me. Vague, uninformative calls rarely got my attention.

Having said that, there are plenty of examples where it pays to leave no stone unturned. Beth, my cohort in the ad process, had more time in her schedule to screen calls than I did. As a result, she often responded to the kinds of marginal ads that I ignored. One of the greatest guys we ever met through the personals was a caller who left almost no personal information at all. Even though he had given scant reason to call, Beth liked his voice, and she noted that his phone prefix was in a nice area of town. She called him back, and he turned out to be a real dream date.

Handsome, successful, a man who had no problem talking at great length in a one-on-one situation. He was just an efficient kind of guy, with better things to do than leave expansive phone messages in someone's voice mailbox. He turned out to be tall, wore Armani suits, and was quite the gracious man-about-town. This was definitely a close encounter. They dated for nearly a year.

The main point is that when you tell your prospects about yourself, it is very likely that they will tell you about themselves in turn. It is up to you whether or not you want to pursue the marginal responses. If you are actively utilizing the personal ad process, you will probably have more than enough qualified prospects without having to follow up on people who haven't given you much information on which to base a decision. Your own time constraints will most likely affect how often you return marginal calls.

Voice mail is an integrated part of this new process of meeting the right person. Use it to balance and expand the brief remarks in your ad. Just as in marketing cars, refrigerators, or even shoes, there is a print medium (newspapers, magazines) and radio promotion. They're elements of a larger marketing plan, and they are designed to support each other. Likewise, your own personal ad is just part of a larger package that includes your voice mail and, later, your interview skills.

PLAN IN ADVANCE TO SOUND GREAT

You're not done just because you've written and placed your ad! Remember — you will enter your voice mailbox as soon as you receive the confirmation and access information for each ad you place. Voice mail is the perfect opportunity for you to tell your prospects more about yourself and more about the kind of person you are looking for. Your message will affect the kinds of responses you receive. It's a very important part of directing your ad to your target, and attracting the desired audience. Some prospects may listen to your ad and not leave a message. Your voice mail message has to make you seem human and accessible — a real person. This is key to how you market yourself.

In personal ads, you are marketing a product, and the product is you. We all understand marketing. We are exposed to it every day — on the radio and TV, on billboards and in newspapers, magazines, and every other medium imaginable. Your outgoing voice mail message is just like a private radio commercial tailored specifically to your prospects. You don't just want the message to be good, you want your private commercial to *sound* good, too.

Sit up straight when you record your voice mail message. Good posture improves the tone and quality of your voice. No one wants to sound tired, bored, or as if they're lying down when they speak. How would you respond to a message recorded by someone with a very soft or weak voice, or someone who mumbles? Sit up and speak clearly!

Portable or cellular phones don't always have the best connection. Be sure you use a phone line free of static to record your outgoing message.

You will want to sound natural and relaxed. If you have a tendency to speak very fast or very slowly, practice adjusting your pace. If you have a high-pitched voice, there are exercises available to help you comfortably speak in a lower range.

Although you will have a limited amount of time to give your presentation — generally two to three minutes — this is plenty of time to get your message across to your prospects. No one wants to listen to overly long messages, anyway.

The good news is, if you make a mistake while you are recording, you can erase it and try again. Many voice mail systems even allow you to modify your message for some period after you have recorded the original version. The systems I have used permitted changes once every twenty-four hours. This gives the publisher the opportunity to monitor your message for use of phone numbers, full names, profanity or other inappropriate items before it is posted to the system.

Above all, make sure that you sketch out some ideas for your message before you record it. This will result in a more impressive message for your callers to listen to. One approach is to outline the items you wish to mention in your message and then just "wing it." This approach works quite well, because your message is extemporaneous and natural-sounding while including key elements you wish to share.

It's important not to come across as phony or too rehearsed.

Keep a naturalness in the quality of your voice — like talking to a friend. Sounding natural makes you accessible, reachable, human.

I actually wrote out my entire message and read it line for line. I practiced reading it to myself at the pace I planned to use, and I underlined words or pauses to add inflection to my script. By inflection, I mean the tone of voice and the attitude that it conveys to the listener. Be positive.

Who wants to listen to a whiny voice describing a litany of people who should not call? "No smoking." "No drinking." "No drugs." If these habits are a problem for you, why not say so in a pleasant way? "I prefer people who do not smoke and drink — it doesn't suit me. I like to select friends who don't use drugs."

Doesn't that say the same thing?

Many of the best public speakers say something early in their presentations to put their audience at ease. A good speaker, like a good teacher, knows that the audience will listen more closely and learn more if they can relate to the speaker. I call this the "gosh" technique. To me, Jimmy Stewart personified this approach in the movies. "...Gosh..."

You can set the tone for such a voice mail message with an ad like:

DARLING BLOND, age 43, petite, successful & nice. Above average mentally, physically, emotionally & spiritually. Seeks magic & love with prosperous companion & potential life mate.

Then follow up with a friendly, engaging voice mail. In the following example of the "gosh" technique, I actually used the word!

Gosh — dating in the '90s — what can I say? If you're at all like me, you're very busy with your successful and interesting career, and it doesn't leave a lot of time for

meeting people. Looks truly are not the most important thing — but they certainly are a blessing, and I'm a very lucky girl. The first thing I look for in companionship, male or female, is intelligence and a positive attitude. I am very busy. In addition to my work, which fascinates and challenges me, I am very involved in the small beach community where I live. I get frequent exercise along the beach, and I have a wonderful lifestyle. I've worked hard to achieve what I have and, frankly, I'm looking for a gentleman of similar accomplishments.

Do leave me a message if you think that is appropriate, and suggest the best time for me to reach you. The best time for me to take personal calls is in the morning, around 7-8 a.m., but I'd be happy to call you at another time...

At this ripe old age, I'm pretty fussy. I think that's fair. Thank you for your time and attention. Leave a message for Darling Blond.

Make sure you are healthy and well rested when you record your message. You won't sound natural, and you definitely won't attract anyone, if you cough after every other word, or if your nasal passages are clogged up. If you are sick, take a week off and wait until you are better to record your message.

THE DENTIST

I have to admit that his voice was not all that impressive. However, his telephone prefix indicated that he lived in the same town as I, and he was a professional. I decided to return his call.

When we talked, he mentioned that he had two children — one of whom was a teenager who still lived at home with him. Although children were not a part of the profile I had developed for my ideal candidate, I made an exception in this case because The Dentist was certainly a man who could afford to support two children.

The Dentist also confided that he had been married only once before — to a ballerina who died young. I guess I should have seen the warning signs when he told me that his home was decorated in ballet-related prints and artwork. We agreed to meet at a local bookstore.

Unfortunately, the meeting started off on the wrong foot. We had originally planned to go for a walk but, when The Dentist arrived, he was still in his work clothes. I, of course, was in shorts and tennis shoes, ready for our walk. Instead, we just talked, and it was quickly apparent to me that he was going to be one more close encounter, but not the man for me.

His tastes were a little too highbrow for me — the opera, the ballet — not that I have anything against them. That's just not my favorite way to spend an evening.

The big problem, however, turned out to be The Dentist's wife. Although she had been dead for years, it was very clear that she held a glorified position in this man's memory. How could I compete against a ballerina who died at the peak of her beauty, poise and health?

He said he would call, but he never did. I will never know why. Maybe his girlfriend was back in town. Or maybe he felt, as I did, that something wasn't quite right. Regardless of the reason, this was another close encounter, and I was as optimistic as ever that I was getting closer to my goal.

My ad was clearly attracting candidates of quality, and my voice mail was successful at encouraging them to leave messages.

CHAPTER 8

Screening and Rating Your Calls

Okay — you've placed your ad, you've recorded your voice mail message, you've set up your notebook and you're starting to get calls. Now what?

It's time to separate the winners from the also-rans — the ones with potential from the ones whose messages you save, but probably will not call back.

In many ways, this is the most important part of the personal ad process. If you abbreviate the process here, you'll work harder than you have to, and you can waste a lot of time interviewing or meeting with prospects who aren't right for you.

Conversely, if you over-screen your prospects, you may overlook someone who would have been a perfect match for you, if you had only taken the time to consider them.

In this chapter, we will consider the best ways to screen and categorize your prospects. You can't possibly call every person who leaves a message in your voice mailbox. You wouldn't want to. Unless you have written your ad very narrowly, you will probably get more calls than you know what to do with.

Be thoughtful when you listen to your messages. What do you think about the caller's voice? Are they sincere, or do they sound a little too slick? Do they meet your criteria? What is your first impression — is this clearly a winner or do you need more convincing? Do they sound like someone you would really like to get to know?

The answers to these questions will determine which prospects you will call back and which will have to continue their searches elsewhere.

IT'S A FAST TRACK

When you start to get your first calls, you'll be delighted just to be getting messages. It's fun! However, after you get over the initial excitement of receiving a message — any message — you'll begin looking for quality rather than quantity.

When you play back your messages, take notes quickly. Voice mail messages go by pretty fast. Jot down the key information in your journal. Name, phone number, major interests, likes, dislikes. If you missed something, you can replay the message, although you probably won't need to. After awhile, you'll get a pretty good feel for the callers who will be good candidates and those who will be rejected. The more practice you have, the more quickly you will be able to size up your callers.

If you stay with the program for an extended period of time, you will probably — as I did — become irritated by the many messages you receive from callers who are way off base. You'll begin to wonder if they even read your ad. Be prepared to be surprised on occasion.

I once returned a call I received from a man only to discover that he was quite a bit younger than the age range my ad specified. When we spoke he admitted that, although he was aware of my age preference, he liked my ad and felt that we would have a lot in common. Maybe this would have been the case — I'll never know for sure. While he was very articulate, and persuasive that we should meet, I told him I would think about it and call him back later. I never did.

With so many calls to choose from — so many opportunities — there is really no reason to compromise your goals. You don't want to be too rigid but, in general, it is much better to stay with your agenda and your priorities. You will have plenty of time to expand your target audience later. Besides, if you are diligently taking notes, you will have Mr. Not-Quite-Right's phone number archived safely away in your journal. You can always call him back if you change your mind.

LISTEN FOR NUANCES

As you are taking notes, carefully listen to the message. I don't mean just hearing what is being said by your caller. I mean really listening. With your head, your heart, your soul — drawing upon your past experiences, your goals, your priorities and whatever wisdom you can bring to bear.

When you are listening to a voice mail message, you have the benefit of not being distracted by the other person's physical presence. You can really focus in on what is being said and how the other person expresses him- or herself.

Listening is a skill that could stand improvement in most of us. In some situations, being a poor listener might not have much of an impact. However, if you hope to accomplish an especially important task (like finding your life-mate!), effective listening skills are a must.

We all have a lot on our minds. Have you ever caught yourself on the phone with someone, and they ask you a question, and you had no idea what they had been talking about for the last five minutes?

When you listen to your messages, devote yourself to the process. Don't shortchange yourself or your callers. Find a time and a place where you can listen to your messages completely and unhurriedly. You might find that a good place and time is at home, after you return from the office, maybe just before you go to bed. Or at work, during your lunch hour.

Find a place where you won't be interrupted and a time when you won't be rushed.

Trust your intuition. If something doesn't feel right about the caller, it probably isn't. Just as importantly, if the caller doesn't hit the target with all of your goals, but you have a feeling that there is something special there, go with your instinct and return his call.

TRUST YOUR FIRST IMPRESSION

It is truly amazing how often your first impression can be the most accurate one. Remember taking multiple choice tests in school? I'm sure you also remember trying to answer a particularly difficult question, and finally making a decision. However, as you thought it over, you decided to change your answer because you were sure that your first choice couldn't be right. Of course, when you got your test back from the teacher with that particular question marked incorrect, you discovered that your first impression was the right one after all.

The same thing happens when you are introduced to new people. Within the first few minutes of meeting, you form a first impression that is very difficult to change. While first impressions can sometimes be wrong, more often than not they are right on target.

Trust your first impressions. You shouldn't have to talk yourself into liking someone or wanting to meet someone. If you find yourself trying to persuade yourself to be interested in one of your callers, step back for a moment and consider your options. Are there other candidates more worthy of your attention right now? What exactly is it that doesn't seem quite right about your caller? Jot down any comments that come to mind — depressed, too young, too old, off target, or even weird.

If, after you have considered your options, you're still not certain what to do, put the caller on your list of people to interview. What can it hurt? Your identity is protected, and you might learn something that will either confirm or override your first impression. Either way, you will be glad that you took the extra time to be absolutely sure about your decision. It only takes a few minutes to call and back out if this is a "no way" candidate.

CHAPTER 8: SCREENING AND RATING YOUR CALLS

My favorite success story is the woman who ran an ad for four years before she found the perfect man. She knew exactly who she was and who she was looking for. Her choice for a life-mate would be of the same faith, he would be willing to make a commitment, have a desire to become married, and would want to raise a family. She got a lot of calls from men who did not measure up to these simple, narrow standards.

Rather than try to mold herself to these callers, she stuck to her guns and refused to deviate from her goals. She screened her calls very strictly and, if they weren't right for her, she simply did not call them back. If she was in doubt, she would call them back, then decline to meet them if her first impressions weren't turned around by her callers.

The point is, she made the choice. She was in control of the situation. She was very clear about what she wanted, and had no desire to experiment. It took a long time, but eventually she found the perfect man — through the personal ads!

REPLAY BEFORE YOU ERASE

Don't forget — once you erase the call, or go on to the next one, it is gone forever. Make absolutely sure that you have gotten all the information you need to make an informed decision. Even though you might be taking notes as quickly as you can, it may be difficult to keep up with a caller — especially if they are excited or just naturally a fast talker. You have the option to replay the message if the name or number was spoken too fast — it's always a good idea to double check.

After you take your notes, but before you erase the message, listen to it one more time and make sure that you have recorded the information accurately.

If you do lose an important piece of information, don't despair. Your caller may call back when you don't return their call, or they may respond if you run a slightly different ad. I have known of cases where a party lost a phone number and placed an ad hoping to re-establish contact with the other party.

SUMMARIZE WHILE IT'S FRESH

Your caller's message will never be as clear in your mind as it is right after you listen to it. Write a brief summary of your thoughts in your journal. Go beyond the key points that you extracted from your caller's message. You might, for example, write something like:

Super attitude, stable career, is confident and has a sense of humor, sounds like a winner, he's a definite call back!

I can guarantee that, after you listen to several messages back-to-back, it will be quite difficult to remember all the nuances of the individual callers. One caller merges into another and, before you know it, you can lose the spark of personality that separates a winner from a loser.

Personality differences can be very subtle and, if you don't make notes of the things you liked and the things you didn't like about the caller immediately after you listen to the message, it will be almost impossible to reconstruct the information later. You may not have time to call back until later that day, or two or three days later. When you do reach them, your personal notes will be your best reference.

RED FLAGS

As you listen to your messages, be on the alert for callers who might be someone other than who they say they are, or who have some motive other than that stated in their message. The intent of the caller may be innocent and they may mean no harm. However, in some very rare cases, the caller may not be on the up and up. Although I am not personally aware of anyone ever having a problem with a caller who was seriously out of line, it is only practical to always exercise common sense and caution — just in case.

I have learned the hard way that prospects use certain buzz words to make them appear more interesting, sexy, or attractive than they really are. For example, I once arranged to meet a man who described himself as looking like Sean Connery. Maybe I was a little naive, but I couldn't help thinking of the dashing, fit and trim secret agent James Bond of '60s movie fame — rescuing his women from all kinds of predicaments.

I should have known better. When we finally met, it turned out that the only thing that this particular prospect had in common with Sean Connery was his bald head.

Similarly, I have learned that, when someone describes himself as being cuddly, it probably means that he is very big. I once went out with a man who described himself as looking like a former football player. I'm sure you're a step ahead of me by now. Instead of the athlete I was expecting to meet, my date really did look like a former football player — he was flabby and overweight.

Many women prefer a tall man. Since my ad did not specify tall, and usually mentioned that I was petite, it was interesting how men would indicate their own height. Almost invariably, my callers said that they were six feet tall. Now, how could that be? It doesn't seem possible that every one of my callers was exactly six feet tall. I suspect that, if they were anywhere near six feet tall — even if they had to stand on their tiptoes — they would round up.

When the gentlemen were definitely not six feet tall, they almost always embellished their height upwards. A couple of times I was absolutely shocked at how small my caller turned out to be. Sometimes I outweighed them!

What can you do to cut through the fluff and get the real story?

CHAPTER 8: SCREENING AND RATING YOUR CALLS

The best way is to ask a few personal questions as you go along — you can even be humorous about it. When your prospect says that he has a lot of hair, it's okay to ask, "Is it on the top of your head?" Say it with a smile.

The single greatest complaint I hear from men using the personal ads is that women will sometimes tell outright lies about their weight. I guess it is just human nature to hope that, once he meets you, your caller will realize how special you are and overlook the discrepancy. My advice is to be forthcoming from the beginning and tell the truth about your weight. If you don't, you are probably setting yourself up for rejection and disappointment.

Other red flags to look for are not as innocent as these attempts to make the caller seem more attractive. These are the kinds of red flags that you have to be particularly watchful for.

You might receive a call from someone who seems to be in too much of a hurry to meet. In a case like this, you'll have to trust your instincts. On one hand, this impatience might be attributable to your caller's excitement about finally having the chance to meet someone he is really interested in. If I were inclined to make an exception and rush to meet, I would be certain to choose a safe, secure location.

What if you receive a call from someone who will only give you their office phone number? If you ask for a home number, they make excuses and put you off. They may have a valid reason to withhold their home phone number, but there may be another reason for this behavior. In a situation like this, it is quite possible that your prospect is married, or has a live-in friend they don't particularly care for you to meet.

Beware the red flags, and keep your guard up — at least until you get to know your prospect a little better. While some red flags may cause no more than mild disappointment or an inward chuckle or two on your part, there is a remote possibility of someone using the personal ads to take advantage of individuals who have run ads. Ask appropriate questions and make sure that you don't rush into anything too quickly.

Listen to your intuition and, if something doesn't feel right, simply go on to the next one — but keep the name and number in your journal. Keeping every name and number is your own assurance that you will know if the same person calls again.

RANKING YOUR CANDIDATES

The amount of time you have available will determine the number of calls that you return. In the beginning, I returned many calls, although I met with only a few of the callers. Later, I developed a good sense of which calls would most likely be of interest, and I returned only those calls.

You decide. Remember, returning a call is not a commitment. It is simply your opportunity to research and interview.

After you listen to your calls, it is important to rank your prospects. The easiest way to do this is to establish three categories of callers: the "definites," the "maybes" and the "no-ways."

The "definites" are candidates who most closely match the profile of the man or woman of your dreams. Understand that it will be the truly uncommon and rare candidate who will match each and every one of the traits you consider to be important in your life mate. These are the prospects who really impress you, and there is no question at all that you will call them back.

During the course of your interview, you will be able to quickly and easily determine whether or not to meet this person, although it is quite likely that you will. With your "definite" prospects, you already know that you are interested, so circle their name or put a star — or three stars — in the margin. Anything to briefly note your interest and their premier ranking.

The "no-ways" are just that. There is no way that you would even remotely consider going out with the people on this list. Maybe these callers are too young or too old. Perhaps they have nothing in common with you, or only one or two things. Whatever the situation, in these cases you won't even bother with an interview because you already know that there is nothing your caller could tell you that would make you change your mind.

Simply draw a quick line through the "who" message or put a No! in the corner of the margin. Be sure to save the note in your journal or record of calls.

The "maybes" are those you are not really sure about. They have some plusses and some minuses. These are candidates you will want to spend some extra time on, deciding if they meet your criteria.

This is where your original notes and impressions are most helpful. They will tilt the balance toward (or away from) returning the prospect's call. You still won't be able to call every one, so be selective.

If you're still wavering, conduct a phone interview before you decide if this is someone you'd like to meet. A question mark near the name or in the margin will remind you to reconsider this candidate before you make a decision one way or the other.

Once you have ranked your prospects, you can return your calls in order of priority. You will, of course, want to call your highest-ranking candidates first — you don't want them to get away before you have a chance to meet them. Once you have made calls to all your definites, you can follow up with the maybes to see if you can convert them into either definites or no-ways.

One last screening technique: If I wanted another impression of a prospect, I sometimes called his number at a time I expected him to be away. It's amazing what you can learn from someone's answering machine!

I often learned more from a man's answering machine than I did by interviewing him. For example, sometimes the answering machine clearly belonged to a bachelor with sole use of the machine, and the message might sound too cool, too jive, too cute for me. Sometimes the machine indicated other names. It is usually fairly easy to determine if these other people are roommates or family members.

These clues, and others like them, can be very useful in helping you screen your candidates. Four male names on a machine sounds to me, right or wrong, like a low-rent flophouse. I'm exaggerating, but it is a clue.

Frequently, the tone of the voice on the answering machine would be dull, even depressed — not at all like the upbeat message they left on my voice mail. Obviously, these callers were putting up a front — hoping that I would be attracted.

It's often difficult to decide who gets a callback. Sometimes a message has several pieces of information that are just okay, neither absolutely in nor absolutely out. The engineer I grew so fond of might never have gotten a callback if he hadn't mentioned his guitar. It gave me another angle from which to view him.

Likewise, another message that seems marginal, okay for age, zip code not great, but sounds satisfactory, might mention a Harley-Davidson motorcycle. This is where your personal selection process kicks in. For me, Harley meant mid-life crisis. Someone else might think "great fun, I hope to meet this guy."

You get to choose, and how much time you have to spend may influence your decisions. Face the fact that sometimes you will overlook a good prospect, and be comforted with the knowledge that you're not wasting time on losers.

In real estate, I have heard the expression "cherry picker." An agent who works only with easy clients who are ready to buy could be called a cherry picker — working only with the ripe ones. I prefer to think of it as the Zen of real estate — the least amount of effort for the maximum results. Efficient.

I confess that I became pretty choosy about who I decided to call back. I felt it was more important to save my energy for the good ones — otherwise I would find myself run ragged by prospects who weren't really interested anyway. The same goes for the personal ads — why waste time and energy? It's much better to look rested and feel ready when the right one shows up.

It's a personal choice, so call as many or as few as you please.

The next part of the process is the interview, and it is an important way to help you determine if you will agree to meet your prospect or not. While your candidate may have passed every test thus far with flying colors, the interview can make or break him. This is where we determine whether or not to meet. The fun begins.

THE LAWYER

This man sounded lively and energetic. His message was so upbeat I found myself interested in him almost immediately. His voice had a lot of spark, and I really liked his attitude.

When I returned his call, I learned he had adult children and that he was at the top of my desired age range. Even so, I knew I had to meet him and find out if there might be a chance for us. We agreed to go out for dinner that later led to dancing, as well.

As I suspected, The Lawyer was a very nice man. Unfortunately, as with The Judge before him, we had an age issue. Despite the fact that he had a lot of energy, I was just not interested in spending the rest of my life with someone who was already nearing the twilight of his.

We had a great time, and he made it very clear that he wanted to see me again soon. I enjoyed our evening together, but I knew that he was not the one for me.

I was aware that he was much more interested in me than I was in him, so I broke off our relationship. He called a few times to see if he could change my mind, but I decided it was far more important to stick with my goals than to take advantage of his good nature and generosity.

Undaunted, I was determined to continue my search until I found the man of my dreams.

CHAPTER 9

Interviewing: A Unique Experience

Fascinating! This is the only way to describe the many different life stories that you will hear on your voice mail system. Soon, you will be sharing your life story with people who are ready to tell you theirs. Some of these stories will be of typical, everyday people. Others will be stories of truly extraordinary men and women.

The interview process provides you with a golden opportunity to learn more about your caller before you commit to a meeting. This really is a new dating ritual — positioning, sharing a little bit of this and a little bit of that — all adding up to a complete package of information that will help you decide who you will take the time to meet. Old social rules and customs are reversed. You are expected to ask personal questions — the same questions that would be impertinent or presumptuous in other circumstances.

You are bound to have many questions to ask — just as your prospect will want to ask you questions. Have you ever been married? What kind of music do you like? Would you like to have children someday? The interview is your opportunity to take the next step toward meeting your goal of finding a life-mate. Only you know what is important to you, and only you know what information you will need to make a decision. Make your questions count.

Sometimes your rating for the callback starts out fine but, as the interview conversation progresses, you learn things that are not good news. It's better to hear these things now rather than later.

One of my conversations started out okay — my candidate was

within my parameters. When we started talking about work and career, he shared a story of being in business with his wife and how, during the divorce, she took over the company and now he worked for her. This sounded a little complicated to me — not a relationship I wanted to get involved with. That was my choice.

In a traditional setting, I might not have learned this information until much later in the relationship.

If there is any step that slows down the personal ad process, it is the interview. Despite this fact, interviewing is a very critical step in the process — one that deserves your full time and attention.

The problem with skipping this step or glossing over it is that your pre-screening will be less effective. You may agree to meet with people you truly have no potential with. This is just not a good use of your time. It is much more efficient to narrow the field in advance — even if it means that you end up with no new prospects for the week.

It is disappointing to take the time to meet someone, only to realize within moments that it was a mistake. Repeated disappointment could cause you to lose faith in the system and drop out of the process.

Men tend to be very eager to meet women — partly because they are visually oriented and partly because they just want to see the woman as early in the process as possible. This is human nature. Even so, you can choose to stick closely to your careful screening process, or you can give a little.

Many of my students have told me that often the men whose messages and personal details are of most interest to them are exactly the men who wish to skip over the phone interview and schedule a meeting. When this happens, and you're curious to meet based on the little information you have, be sure to select a location convenient for you to keep the process efficient for time and energy.

When you meet, continue to interview live and in person. It really is easier to ask these personal questions on the phone beforehand — but either way, they must be asked. It's natural to feel self-conscious, but just focus on the other person. Be clear in your mind about what you need to ask, then take your mind off yourself (what you're wearing, how you sound), relax and have a good time.

Even if you have had lengthy personal discussions before you meet, the first encounter is your next best opportunity to continue to ask qualifying questions. If you pass up this opening and still decide to see more of each other, you are basically back to the old dating ways. It may take you years to discover the essential details that can make or break the relationship.

Sometimes, if someone sounded particularly interesting, I broke my own rule about knowing all the facts and I would agree to meet — as long as we met near my home or office. That way, I might be disappointed, but at least I wasn't exhausted, too.

Fortunately, it only takes a little time, and a commitment to the interview process, to reduce the wrong turns in your search for a lifemate. Listen to every clue, nuance or bit of information you can gain from your prospect.

We all make mistakes. Sometimes you will agree to meet the wrong person. However, while you are screening and selecting, it is good to allow for some flexibility. Sometimes you have to follow your heart. If he doesn't meet all your criteria, but your heart tells you that there is something special about a prospect, by all means meet them. You may end up wasting an hour of your time, but maybe you will find the person you will spend the rest of your life with.

REMEMBER — THEY ASKED YOU TO CALL

The ball is in your court. You placed your ad, and now you are getting responses to it. You are about to meet some very interesting and special people — people who, like you, are hoping to meet some-

CHAPTER 9: INTERVIEWING — A UNIQUE EXPERIENCE

one to share their hopes and dreams with. They read your ad, they listened to your voice mail message, and they found in you a kindred spirit — someone they want to get to know better.

Now it's your turn. It's time to take the next step on your journey — a step that will lead you into a lifelong partnership with someone you really care about — and who really cares about you.

Interviewing the man or woman of your dreams can be both exciting and a time of some anxiety and trepidation. Some people are more comfortable on the phone than others, and it's very natural to feel reluctant to make those first few return calls. It might be helpful for you to remember that they asked you to call them. They were interested in your ad and your voice mail message. They saw the potential spark and they called you. They want to hear from you!

They are probably just as anxious about the prospect of talking to you as you are about talking to them. It's important that you get past your nervousness so you can communicate with your prospect clearly, intelligently, and with a full understanding of each other.

Up to this point, your callers do not have your phone number or even your first name. Frankly, I was initially uncomfortable leaving my name and my home phone number on an answering machine when I returned messages. I was very cautious — perhaps overly so. In the beginning, I would say that I would call back later, or I would just hang up without leaving a message.

Before you start calling your prospects for interviews, you will have to decide whether you will leave a message on their answering machine. And, too, how their machine sounds may affect your message. "I'm returning your call regarding my ad in the *Reader*, and you can reach me at 555-1234. Please ask for Mary."

My stalwart cohort and personal ad partner, Beth, went so far as to leave fake names when she encountered an answering machine. Needless to say, this became very confusing very fast. If you choose to date your prospect, you're going to have to give your real name at some point! On more than one occasion, Beth was out for a meeting using her assumed nom *de plume*, and a friend greeted her by her real name. To say she was embarrassed would be a serious understatement! Maybe your prospect will understand your reasons for giving a false name, but this is probably not the best way to start out a relationship.

We all make snap judgments and instant evaluations every day. We judge everything from our impression of the attendant at the gas station down the street to our waiter at dinner last night. We pick up much more information than we are consciously aware of. We register how a person moves, any accent of speech and the rhythm and speed at which they respond. We constantly and instantaneously take in and digest all kinds of information about other people all the time.

When you listen to your voice mail, and when you interview your prospect, be in tune to his or her nuances — what is said and what is left unsaid. Listening to a voice on your voice mail heightens and focuses your ability to read between the lines. Their voice, their choice of words and how they express themselves will tell you a lot about your caller.

You will soon find yourself liking or disliking certain calls. That's okay. Taste is a very personal thing. As you decide who to call back, listen to your heart and stay in touch with your innermost feelings. When deciding to return calls, you should respond naturally and choose the calls that you find most intriguing, or those with which you are most comfortable. You are in the driver's seat. You can call back as many or as few people as you like.

THE NEW ETIQUETTE

Understand that personal ads turn the standard process of meeting someone upside-down and topsy-turvy. If you meet someone through work or through friends, it may take you weeks, months, even years to learn the intimate details of their lives.

When you first meet someone, it's not polite to ask too many questions at once. You certainly avoid any controversial topics like politics or religion. It would be impolite to ask, "How many times have you been married?" But aren't these exactly the kinds of things you need to know about a potential mate? Over a long period of time, as you get to know each other, you find out things like what this person's aspirations are, if they want to have children, if they mix well socially, if they prefer rock music or opera, if they are interested in marriage.

Personal ads are different. Not only do you have the opportunity to ask personal questions, you are expected to. It is perfectly appropriate to ask intimate questions that you wouldn't even consider asking someone you just met. Here, on the phone *before* you even meet, you are invited — indeed encouraged — to ask pertinent questions. It's done casually and comfortably — like talking to a friend. But you get all the facts! It's a great beginning and a great way to save time and disappointment.

Start by going over the list of desired attributes for your life-mate that you wrote down in your notebook. Then write down questions designed to determine if your prospect meets these requirements. This will form the basis for your interview.

Refer to your list of questions often while you're on the phone — it will help keep you on track. If you're uncomfortable taking quick notes as you interview, write down your impressions and important answers in your notebook immediately afterwards.

Focus your questions on essential issues. If religious or political beliefs are important to you, be sure to ask about them. Be direct. "Are you a religious person?" "Do you attend services regularly?" "What party do you belong to?" "Have you done volunteer work for a candidate?" If you have small children, or want children, get right to

CHAPTER 9: INTERVIEWING — A UNIQUE EXPERIENCE

the point: "Do you enjoy children?" "How do you feel about starting a family (or a second family)?"

Don't waste your time on small talk. This is an interview, not a cocktail party.

Try to ask questions that lead to other questions that lead to more information. If the answer is yes to "Have you been married before?" you can follow up with questions about the previous marriage and how it affects your prospect now.

Be interested. People like to talk about themselves, and once you get them talking, you can learn a lot.

The conventional wisdom is that the best ways to meet people are to be involved in the community, join groups, or volunteer. Eventually, or so the belief goes, you're going to meet people and, with a little luck, you will finally come across someone who meets your needs. I belonged to more committees, volunteered for more organizations and was on more boards of directors — anything from the Modern Art Council to the Del Mar Village Merchants Association — than anybody I know. There's no question that I met a lot of men. I had many friends, and they introduced me to every single man they could find. But they had no way of knowing what these gentlemen wanted, what their background was, or if they were already seeing somebody.

In social situations like this, it's just not polite to ask your new acquaintance if they own their own home, or why they got divorced or if they are ready to settle down.

Personal ads change all that. Take advantage of this new dating ritual. Ask personal questions. It's better to find out if you are not potentially compatible with each other now rather than later.

This is not a guarantee that you have immediately found the perfect person. But it is a fabulous opportunity to screen for basic compatibility.

The telephone interview process works both ways. Now is your chance to shine. Don't be shy. If you are an accomplished businessperson, say so. If your idea of a great evening is one spent curled up with a good book, don't hesitate to provide that information.

Above all, be honest and be yourself. Everyone has something beautiful about them. It may be your personality or your looks. It might be your wit or intellect.

The people who are most often disappointed with personal ads are those who try to be someone they aren't. Be yourself, your best self, and I promise that you will get great results.

YOU'RE IN CONTROL

One of the best things about personal ads is that you are in control of the process. You place the ad. You record the voice mail message. You listen to the responses, wherever and whenever you decide to. And you decide who to call back.

As you can see, you really do have full control over who you decide to meet, and the terms of your meeting. If you don't like what you hear — just thank your caller and say good-bye. It's that simple.

If you want to start a family and your candidate doesn't, isn't it better to find out early on instead of later? If you're pleasantly plump and they have a weight fetish, do you really want to see their face fall when you walk through the door?

Before you ever meet, you can get answers to all kinds of basic questions. During your discussion, you can get a feel for attitudes, beliefs, goals and lifestyle. Don't be afraid to ask specific questions. Virtually no subject is taboo, as long as you ask in fairness and honest curiosity.

You can't learn everything on the phone, but you can easily screen out the obviously incompatible. Take full advantage of the New Etiquette by interviewing before you meet.

Wouldn't it be wonderful to spend your time with someone who shares your interests and who really likes you?

However, it can be a mistake to over-screen. Take a few risks. Stretch yourself occasionally — maybe you will learn to like motorcycle riding. Opera? Well, maybe that, too. Focus on the important issues, and be flexible on the minor ones.

PERSONAL INFORMATION ADDS UP

What are you really looking for in a relationship? If you are like most of us, you are probably trying to find someone you will be compatible with — someone with whom you can share a healthy relationship. With the information you obtain from your interview, you can get a pretty strong indication of compatibility. And, while chemistry can work its wonders even across the phone lines, you can be much more objective with your prospect than you would be in a face-to-face situation. Later, if you meet and decide to spend more time together, you may find that you share a strong attraction. However, if you are looking for a relationship that will last, let chemistry follow, not lead.

Personal information adds up. Is your prospect laid-back, or lazy? There is a big difference! Are they selfish and self-absorbed, or just self-confident? The answer to this question could make all the difference in the world to you and to your long-term happiness. Do they want the same things you do, or are they just trying to please you?

It's better to find out their true motivations now, before you get in too deep.

Look for the kind of information that will help you evaluate your reasons whether or not to meet with this person. That is the whole point of the interview process and the New Etiquette. It is your opportunity to determine if your caller is someone you should meet or someone you should pass on.

Oddly enough, you might find yourself procrastinating at this stage — particularly when the meeting might be with the man or woman of your dreams.

If you don't use the interview process to your best advantage, or don't provide an opportunity for your prospects to disclose personal details about themselves, you're not using the ads to their full potential.

You might run a personal ad with broad parameters merely to meet new people, and you might decide not to emphasize the interview portion of the personal ad process. There's nothing wrong with that. However, if you are seriously looking for someone to spend the rest of your life with, you are going to shortchange yourself if you don't conduct serious and thorough interviews.

The interview allows you to learn more about your prospect in advance, before you meet. Wouldn't you rather find out that you are incompatible now, before you meet, than five minutes into a three-hour dinner date? Or worse yet, six weeks or six months later?

First impressions can be pretty interesting. My partner Beth was not terribly impressed with her first exposure to the man she now finds enthralling. Even so, she felt that there might be something there, so she kept in touch with him. Although she saw him occasionally, he was not a priority in her life.

Why was Beth so lukewarm in her response? Perhaps her initial reaction had something to do with the fact that her former husband and the men she had dated since her divorce all had dominant personalities. Beth's new friend is quite gentle in his mannerisms and in appearance. Luckily, it didn't take long for chemistry to work its wonders, and for Beth to warm up to this man. Beth found out that what she thought she wanted and what she really wanted were two completely different things.

As you gather personal information, you need to try to determine what is really important to you. Don't let the fog of past relationships blind you to the kind of person, or type of lifestyle, that would make you as happy as you possibly can be. Sweep away the past and start with a clean sheet. You may be surprised to find, just as my friend Beth did, that the man or woman of your dreams is standing there — right next to you.

Personal ads are the art of the possible, a vision of what could be. This is an opportunity to redefine yourself, even re-invent yourself, who you are and what you seek.

THE INTERVIEW

When you are ready to interview one of your callers, find a quiet place and choose a time when you won't be rushed or interrupted. You will want to concentrate on the answers to your questions, and you don't want to appear to be in too much of a hurry to get the call over with. Hopefully you remembered to use your voice mail to ask your callers to indicate in their messages the best time to call them back. We all have busy lives, so it's not uncommon for days to go by before you reach each other.

To start your interview, I suggest that you begin on a positive note. You could, for example, say something along the lines of "I was pleased to receive your message. Have you had any success with the personal ads? How long have you used them?"

Each conversation will have its own ebb and flow. Start with general topics such as hobbies, local events, or places. You will find that your prospect, too, is interested in talking about career, past relationships and marriages. From the early responses to these questions, you can decide whether or not you wish to continue the interview.

You should expect the question of where each of you lives to come up early in the conversation. If your prospect asks where you live, you can describe the neighborhood or area you live in (don't use your street name or address) and add "I'm so glad I bought this home

CHAPTER 9: INTERVIEWING — A UNIQUE EXPERIENCE

when I did," or "I've lived here for several years, and I really hope to buy in this area!"

While you are on the topic of home ownership, your caller may volunteer whether he owns or rents his home. If he is not specific, you can let it pass or you can go back to that topic with a follow-up question. Frankly, but non-judgmentally ask, "Do you own or rent?" While the answer to this question may not be that important to you, it was particularly important to me in my search for a life partner.

The key is to be non-manipulative — it's all in how you say it.

You may be uncomfortable asking such forward questions, so look for ways to soften the message. When I was new to real estate, it was very difficult for me to ask a client, "How much money do you have?" Indeed, that does sound brazen, but I needed to know before I let them fall in love with a home they couldn't afford. Instead, I learned to ask, "Have you set aside deposit funds for this purchase?"

It's a good idea to give your caller your first name. If you decide to schedule a meeting, you should also consider giving them your home phone number so they can reach you if there is a change in plans. However, if you are highly visible or prominent in your community — like the city councilwoman who came to me for training — then by all means use discretion! The city councilwoman's solution was to give out the unlisted number in her home office. This was an extra line and not the main phone line into her home.

You might choose to give them the phone number of the place where you're going to meet, so they can call if they've been delayed.

Don't forget that you are in control of the interview process. Be honest, even candid. If your prospect presses you for more information, and for any reason you are uncomfortable in providing it, simply say, "I would rather tell you more after we meet." Again, this specifically applies to your home address and where you work.

Note your reactions to the phone interview in your journal. Make sure you've covered your list of questions before you agree to meet a prospect. Write down any other questions that occur to you later, as well as pertinent information about your caller. If you do decide to meet, these notes will come in very handy.

Above all, listen to your own response or inner voice. Just wrap up calls that aren't going well. There are plenty more prospects out there, and you don't need to pursue someone who is not right for you.

If, by chance, you engage someone in conversation and you realize they're not the right person for you, wrap up the conversation early. Be polite, but be firm. If the caller already has your number, you can even indicate that you will be out of town for some time to visit your family. If they don't have your phone number, so much the better.

Some of your conversations will be brief, others may last for hours. I recall many an evening sitting outdoors on my patio with my remote phone — enjoying a lengthy dialogue about past marriages, choices made, philosophies, childrens' progress reports and the challenges and joys of life.

Even when it was apparent that my caller wasn't the man for me, I learned a great deal from these conversations. I learned how they felt, and how they dealt with life. Often, I felt sad about declining to meet with them, but I always tried to express my thanks and support for them in the search for their life-mate.

If you think you might communicate better at another time, but you want to leave the door open to your prospect, then promise to call back.

If at any point you realize that your prospect is a "no go," simply wrap up the conversation.

If you're uncomfortable with the idea of leaving your caller in the lurch, say that someone is at the door, or give them some other excuse for saying good-bye.

BE PREPARED TO SHARE SIMILAR DETAILS

Be open. Share personal details about yourself. It's part of the even exchange that takes place with the phone interview. You have the right to ask, and so does your prospect. If you are open and sharing, it is much more likely that your prospect will be open and sharing, too. Anticipate how you will describe your situation, including your age, appearance, job, past relationships, even your philosophy on life.

Be ready to answer the same questions you plan to ask your candidates. If you want to know more about their former marriages, or why they never married (a very pertinent question, by the way), then you should expect to share similar information.

All of us have had some disappointment or other in life, and many of us have had the occasional failure. There is nothing wrong with this. If you are divorced, then evidently something went wrong. How will you tell this story? What will your story sound like to someone hearing it for the first time? Will you come across as a positive person or a negative one? Do you hold yourself blameless — as someone who believes that everything that went wrong with your life was someone else's fault — or do you freely admit your mistakes, learn, and move on?

Listen to what *you* say. Are you the kind of person *you* would like to meet?

Everything in life is relative. What might be failure in your eyes may be strength of character in the eyes of your beholder. I recall one gentleman who candidly shared with me the details of his prior success story, his devastating divorce, the loss of his company, having to start all over again, and his optimism for his new entrepreneurial efforts.

Instead of being turned off by these apparent failures in this man's life, I was drawn to his obvious personal strength and his ability to grow and learn from his mistakes.

TRUTH, FICTION, AND EMBELLISHMENT

Be forewarned — men and women who use the personal ads tend to embellish their ads just a bit. It's not that these people are lying — usually they are just putting a positive spin on what is basically the truth.

While you are interviewing a prospect, your best indication of whether they are telling the truth or not is their voice. Listen for the little nuances, the pauses, the changes in tone that will indicate that your candidate is exaggerating or even lying.

Do what you wish with this information. Ultimately you decide, but I guarantee that every piece of information you can obtain about a prospect will help you make a better decision.

Whatever you do, it will be worth your while to separate the fact from the fiction *before* you meet — not after!

THE ENGINEER

The Engineer was, without a doubt, one of the nicest men I met in the two years I was active in the personal ad market. I met him through one of my "dynamic blond petite" ads.

Interestingly enough, he didn't sound like an executive to me — he spoke with a soft voice and he had a slight lisp. However, his voice mail message indicated that he was the president of a small company, his home was in an exclusive area and he said that he played guitar and enjoyed blues and country music. Although I definitely was not impressed with his message, the zip code was a very positive indicator, and the part about his playing guitar made me think that he might have a creative side that would balance the analytical, engineer mentality. I was curious.

I called him back and we had a very nice conversation. It turned out that he had been married once, and that it was three years since his divorce. He said he was looking for a long-term relationship and he hoped to eventually marry again. I decided to take a chance and we agreed to meet.

When I first saw him, I was somewhat disappointed. The Engineer was dressed casually — not casual chic, just casual. He was not very impressive physically. In fact, he was a small person, but he was fit from hours of tennis, and he had a healthy glow about him. We had a delightful conversation. The Engineer was obviously goal-oriented but, at the same time, he was nice.

As we walked back to our cars and said goodnight, I instinctively reached out to touch his hand. He later told me that this small, but sincere, gesture made a real difference to him.

The Engineer had called my ad previously, but had not left a message — he felt intimidated by my description of myself. When I touched his hand, he knew that I wanted him to call me back, and my gesture gave him the confidence he needed to call.

We spent six happy months together. During this time, I learned that he had been deeply hurt by his divorce, and that he felt he had been taken advantage of in the financial settlement. He said that he wanted to marry again, but my instincts told me that it would be a long time before The Engineer would be emotionally ready to take the plunge. He never wanted children and, in spite of my obvious ability to support my own children, he viewed them as unattractive accessories.

When I did broach the subject of marriage, it became clear that the first step for him would be to live together. This, however, was not acceptable to me since I already had two teenage children and I had raised them with traditional beliefs and values. I couldn't set this kind of example for them.

I had no choice but to stop seeing The Engineer. This was a very painful time for me, because I cared very much for him. I just didn't think the odds were good. Maybe I could outwait him, maybe not. In retrospect, it would have been a good idea to maintain a relationship with him, but to keep interviewing at the same time.

Sometimes you have to close a door for other doors to open. I still felt that there was one man out there who wanted to marry me — the right man. Not one I would have to coax to the altar, but one who would join with me in joy and commitment.

MAXIMUM RESULTS

When I went back to the ads after my six-month relationship with The Engineer, I didn't want him to know that I was already back in the personal columns where I had met him. So I had a neighbor do my voice mail for me. She is a bit younger than I am and generally at home caring for her young son. This meant she was easy to locate when I needed her help. I also selected her because she was willing to help and she had a very nice voice that was not unlike my own speech.

If you ever use a substitute voice mail assistant, try to find someone who sounds similar to you. Later, when you return messages, it is highly unlikely that anyone will notice the difference. My neighbor turned out to be so good at the voice mail messages that I wish I had used her all along.

As you may recall, I made a practice of placing more than one ad in a publication, even though publishers frown on this. I used my home address and office address. Placing multiple ads is not necessary to achieve excellent results, but it is a technique you might consider. If you use a friend or neighbor as your alternative address, make certain it is someone who checks their mail daily, since the amount of time between receiving your ad confirmation and your voice mail box number is often quite short.

I used whatever resources available to cross-reference my top-ranking candidates. One time, I returned a call to a lawyer whose voice mail message indicated that he was definitely within my target goals for age, career, and even no children. When I interviewed him on the phone, he described a life of high achievement and education. He then proceeded to tell me that he no longer practiced law, that he now focused his energy on writing in the areas of business and investments.

This all sounded okay, but something about the package just didn't ring true.

By now you may think I have a hang-up on where people live and whether they own their own home. Perhaps I do. Personally, I feel it is a strong indicator of lifestyle, aesthetics, maturity and economic success.

The lawyer told me he owned his own home in La Costa. Like most neighborhoods, La Costa has a reputation. When I think of La Costa, I think of older people and families. There are exceptions to this general rule, but my reaction was, "Why does a successful attorney/writer choose to live in La Costa?" He suggested meeting, but I begged off and said I would have to check my schedule – I would get back to him.

The next day, when I was at my office, I thought I would take a minute to confirm where the lawyer lived. I pulled out the office copy of the area cross directory. If you've never seen a copy of a cross directory, it's a very large catalog of phone numbers, in numerical order. In another section of the directory, phone numbers are listed in order of street names and numbers. Every community has a cross directory, and most larger libraries will have a copy in the reference department.

Since your callers have to leave their phone numbers for you to call them back, it's easy to go to a cross directory and look up their address. I discovered that the lawyer lived in a very small condo on a noisy, busy street – not a desirable or valuable location at all.

CHAPTER 9: INTERVIEWING — A UNIQUE EXPERIENCE

Right or wrong, I decided this was not a man I cared to meet. For all I knew, he might have a huge savings hidden away in mutual funds, but I drew my own conclusion.

I'm not suggesting that you take the time to cross reference every candidate that you interview and consider meeting. I do strongly encourage using whatever resources you have available to double check the people you allow to enter your life. Screening for zip code or phone prefix is a practical way to edit your list. Often you may already know someone who works in their office or profession, and a casual follow-up is not inappropriate.

Sometimes additional information is simply not available — your prospect may be new to the area. I probably did fail to meet with some people who might have been possibilities, but there is only so much time and energy to devote to this adventure.

CHAPTER 10

Important Rules for the First Meeting

It's the moment of truth. You're finally going to meet the man or woman of your dreams.

Well, maybe. If you've done your job in the interview process, chances are you will have an interesting meeting — perhaps even a great one. While your candidate may have so far passed the initial screening, your meeting will introduce a new element to the equation — the physical presence and potential chemistry that puts the spark in love and in life.

In this chapter, we will consider the different aspects of this most important step in using the personal ads. You control if, when, and where you meet your callers. We will discuss the importance of choosing a place to meet that is comfortable for you, and the other factors that go into the decision of where to meet. We will consider the clues to watch for that will help you decide if you should pursue a prospect, and how to show him or her that you are interested. Finally, we will discuss how to handle disappointment.

MEET ON YOUR TERMS

The wonderful thing about personal ads is that they allow you to be in control of who you interview and, ultimately, who you decide to meet. You also control *where* you will meet. If you choose a place you are familiar with, and where you are comfortable, you will be much more relaxed than if you meet your new acquaintance in a place where you have never been.

The place you meet tells your candidate something about you. It speaks volumes about the kind of person you are and the kind of person you are looking for.

Dan read the personal ads — he even called a few — but he didn't think they were his cup of tea. However, following my seminar, he decided to place his first ad.

YOUNG 46, fun-loving and fit seeks white female 40-55 who shares interests in music, dancing, outdoors, walks, movies, travel, communication. East County.

Dan's ad was very straightforward — no puffery, no fancy embellishment — just the facts. Indeed, it attracted just the kind of woman Dan realized was likely to enjoy the same lifestyle he did.

Dan frequently met his interviewees at a Denny's restaurant close to his home. He had several reasons for his choice of meeting places. Denny's was easy to find and parking was virtually unlimited. There were always people coming and going — making it a great place to talk to each other privately without being overheard by the rest of the restaurant. There was an additional reason that made Denny's his obvious choice. Dan knew that any woman who objected to meeting him at Denny's was not going to appreciate his lifestyle, either!

Dan dated through the personal ads for a year before he met Diana. Today, they are married and very happy. They have shared countless hikes, camping trips and even a journey to remote Mexican waterfalls. These were not expensive getaways, but enjoyment and oneness made them extremely rich in pleasure.

THE PERFECT PLACE TO MEET

Before you ever meet with any of your callers, give serious consideration to where you might meet. The most important thing is to meet at a place that is convenient to you — somewhere within five or

CHAPTER 10: IMPORTANT RULES FOR THE FIRST MEETING

ten minutes of your home or your office. If you are close to your home or office, and you haven't gone out of your way to get to your meeting, you will be much better able to cope with any disappointment and chalk your meeting up to experience. If you are stuck in traffic for half an hour, it's pretty easy to get frustrated and lose your faith in the ad process. If it's only ten minutes to your home, you can relax and make the best of the situation.

Choose a place that is neither too quiet nor too hectic. If the place is too quiet, you'll feel as if you're on a stage and everyone can hear every word that you speak. Conversely, if it's too crowded, you may have to yell at each other to be heard. Depending on the time of day that you agree to meet, different places can have completely different environments. A bar that is dead as a stone at lunch can be a raucous madhouse during happy hour. Scout your locations in advance and be sure that they meet your needs.

Consider what will work for you — lunch? Before work? After work? Saturday or Sunday coffee? A walk in the park?

Make sure your chosen location can be easily found with clear, straightforward directions. You don't want your date to get lost or be late because they couldn't find the obscure place you selected for your meeting. It's a great advantage to have the phone numbers of the three to five places you're most likely to meet. Your prospect can always call there for better directions or to let you know if they are delayed.

Choose a place where it is unlikely that you will encounter friends or acquaintances. It can be more than a little awkward introducing someone you barely know. Worse, while you are awaiting the arrival of your date, a friend might engage you in conversation and show no sign of leaving. What will you say then? Will your date recognize you, since you will no longer be alone? You can easily avoid these problems by selecting the right places to meet.

CHAPTER 10: IMPORTANT RULES FOR THE FIRST MEETING

Fortunately for me, I had numerous coffee houses and casual cafes to choose from. Alternatively, meeting at a park or similar outdoor spot can be a good choice. Most people feel relaxed going for an unhurried walk.

Be prepared to give clear directions as well as the address and phone number of the place where you will meet. Keep those phone numbers in your notebook for easy access.

I eventually settled on a restaurant that was a virtual landmark in my town. Even people from outside my neighborhood knew of it and where it was located. Since my friends didn't hang out there, it was a perfect place to meet my candidates. It was close to home, safe, familiar, and easy for my dates to find, plus it had valet parking! A date doesn't get much more convenient than that. The places you choose to meet your prospects should offer the same benefits to you.

Just one more detail. How will you recognize each other when you arrive at your meeting place? Unfortunately, there is no sure-fire, easy solution to this problem. We each try to give a description or clues that will help us stand out in a crowd, but often our verbal picture will not be so obvious to the one looking for us. I remember telling The Dentist that I had a lot of long, blond hair. I don't know exactly what he was expecting, but evidently it was more blond or more hair. Likewise, I was expecting to go for a walk, but he was still dressed in his office clothes. Eventually, we did find each other, but it was not a smooth beginning.

It is common to tell your date that you will be wearing a certain color. This is fine until the weather changes and the dress or coat you were planning to wear is all wrong for the meeting. It can get confusing very quickly. Regrettably, I don't have a specific recommendation to avoid this floundering. However, I encourage you to consider in advance how you will facilitate the recognition of each other.

For a woman, a colorful scarf that can be easily removed might be the ticket. For a man, it might be a pair of sunglasses tucked into a jacket pocket. So often, our physical descriptions — moustache, brown hair, average height — are very common. You can walk into almost any room and see several people who meet the same description. Do whatever you can to make yourself stand out. It will make your initial meeting much smoother.

SIGNS TO WATCH FOR

It's really amazing what you can discover about someone on your first date. You can find out about their attitude toward work — is it drudgery or is it an exciting challenge? You can find out about their attitude towards money.

You will quickly discover if your date understands the niceties of life. For example, it's traditional for the man to pick up the tab, and this is a tradition that I personally like. It's a very old custom whereby a man first expresses his interest and demonstrates it by paying for the food or entertainment. Not only is this courteous, but it is a great way to start a relationship.

When you are meeting for your first date, it will often be only for coffee or cocktails. In this case, it's not really a traditional date — just a first meeting. If you are a woman, be prepared to pay for your own drink. Most men will offer or even insist on paying this modest sum. However, you should be prepared to pay your own way, and you should offer to.

If the meeting is scheduled for lunch or dinner, decide in advance if you can comfortably afford to pay your own way. Frankly, I maintain a pretty strict budget. As a single mother of two teenage children, lunch or dinner out was a special occasion. If my caller suggested that we meet over lunch or dinner at a pricey location, I let him know my preference by saying "I'm on a bit of a budget now. It would be better if we met for coffee." This works for men, too. You don't want to give your date the impression that you have deep pockets — even, or perhaps especially, if you do.

I once had a tiny misunderstanding in this area. I always made a point of offering to pay my own way. Since I didn't have the money to waste on lunches and dinners out, this meant a lot of meetings over coffee or cocktails. One of my interviewees insisted on meeting for lunch, even though I tried to steer the arrangements toward "just coffee." The lunch was fine, but the company was dreadful! The more I learned about this gentleman, the less I liked him. His stories of his life, his family, and his relatives indicated that he was incredibly selfish and self-centered and, in my eyes, he had insufficient grounds for such a high opinion of himself!

When it came time to pay the bill, he indicated that we should share the cost of lunch. Now, we weren't talking about a lot of money, but his attitude had gotten my goat and brought out the stubborn streak in me. So I told him, "You insisted on lunch. As I recall, I really preferred to meet just for coffee, so I assumed I would be your guest."

He paid the bill. I wasn't proud of myself for my behavior — I would much rather have avoided the situation altogether.

Sometimes your date will convey revealing bits of personality in their comments about the menu, or in the way they analyze the check, or in how graciously and generously they leave a tip. These may be isolated incidents, but if your impression of your date as a tightwad, a cheapskate or a big spender repeats itself, you should consider what this means to you in a potential relationship.

There are other signs to watch for besides the size of the tip that he leaves. Does he like kids? If he is divorced, what does he now think about the institution of marriage? Is he a little too rough for your tastes, or a little too slick? Does he seem to like the same kinds of things, and does he share the same kinds of values that you do? Is he interesting or dull, funny or boring? Is this person someone you would enjoy spending another evening with, let alone the rest of your life?

Your first date is the best time to continue the interview process. Before you meet, go over your notes, see if you have any unanswered questions or concerns. Use the New Etiquette to get the information you need. Later it will become more awkward to ask sensitive questions. And, as chemistry begins to weave its magic, you're less likely to want to ask the difficult questions. Do it now.

Regardless of who has the higher income and who pays the bills, the other person should always reciprocate in some way. If your resources are stretched, there are still many ways for you to show your appreciation. A home-cooked meal, a picnic, even a pizza is welcome. It's not the money that's important — it's the fact that you took the time to show your interest and consideration for the other person. You can avoid misunderstandings by letting your partner know what your situation is, and what you would like to do in return. Honesty and openness pay off.

GIVE A GESTURE IF INTERESTED

When I first met with The Engineer, we had a great conversation and a pleasant evening together. Still, it wasn't until we bid each other good night and I reached out to touch his hand that he felt certain that I was interested in him. I hadn't planned to do that, but if I hadn't communicated my interest in a way that he could clearly understand, he might not have called me back.

There are many ways to show your date that you are interested, and that you would like to continue your relationship. Perhaps the most direct way is to tell your date that you enjoyed your meeting and you would like to see him or her again. If you phrase this in terms that don't push your prospect into a corner, it can be a welcome signal to the other party. For example, you could say, "I had a lovely evening. I hope that we'll have the opportunity to get together again soon." You have clearly shown your interest, and you have left the door open for another meeting.

In addition to saying that you are pleased to meet your date, consider your choice of a parting gesture. Perhaps a hug would work for you, or maybe a hand on your partner's shoulder or a touch of his hand. Be willing to give an extra signal of encouragement. Otherwise, they might wonder if you're just being polite.

Whatever you decide, your gesture should be sincere and from the heart. If you are sincere in your feelings, the message will be received loud and clear by your partner. There will be no confusion in their mind about where they stand. If they are interested, they will be sure to call you back.

BE GENEROUS OF HEART WHEN DISAPPOINTED

Face it. There will be times when you interview a prospect who seems quite promising. When you talk on the phone, there is a comfortable rapport — you can relate to each other, and your questions are answered satisfactorily. You like what you hear and you are curious to meet. Then, when you walk in the room and they rise to greet you, your heart falls from its usual perch high in your chest to the bottom of your stomach.

It took me two years to find my husband through the personal ads. During that time, I met many very wonderful men. However, I had my share of disappointments, too. If you spend any time at all with the personal ads, you will experience frequent disappointment. It's nothing to worry about. It happens to everyone.

Some meetings will be totally wrong. Others will be near-misses. It's a numbers game, and that's how you increase the odds of finding the one person who is right for you. Believe me, you will face disappointment more often than not. Plan to hang in for the duration — it takes time. Sometimes months — sometimes years.

CHAPTER 10: IMPORTANT RULES FOR THE FIRST MEETING

The question is, how do you handle yourself when you are disappointed? My personal advice is to be as gracious and as generous as you possibly can be.

Don't forget that your date has feelings, and they probably have a lot of anticipation and dreams riding on their meeting with you. When you interviewed them, you felt something that attracted you. You should be able to find some common areas of conversation. Go ahead and spend twenty minutes, an hour, or whatever time you can spare.

I have made several dear friends of men who didn't live up to my expectations. Although I wasn't attracted to them in a romantic sense, I still enjoyed their company, and I still liked what was on the inside. Take time to talk with your date — they took the time to see you.

The key is not to rush to judgment. Haven't we all, at one time or another, been surprised at who we enjoy spending time with? Maybe it's a co-worker from the office, or maybe it's a neighbor. You appear to have little in common but, despite this fact, you become fast friends.

I didn't spot Beth as a potential friend for quite awhile. My neighbor Joe and I probably look a little like the Odd Couple at first glance, but we have worked hard to keep our local TV series on the air and we have grown close as a result. I value Joe's insight and our friendship. It was Joe who encouraged me to try the personal ads, and I have him to thank for introducing me to this fabulous opportunity. What a friend he has turned out to be!

While you may sometimes know within seconds or minutes whether someone is right for you or not, it usually will take some time.

In the next chapter, we will discuss how to recognize the right man or woman for you, and how to be sure that you don't overlook a great opportunity.

THE MISTAKE

I should have known better. When I was using the personal ads, I had a rule to meet my prospects in locations that were within ten minutes of my home. That way, I wouldn't have far to go if things didn't work out. This time, however, I made an exception.

Our phone conversation had gone really well. This gentleman seemed like a great guy — intellectual, very well-informed, creative. He lived an hour away from me, but he seemed so interesting on the phone, I agreed to meet him halfway. Once I arrived, I wasted at least ten minutes searching for a place to park. I finally found a parking space, quickly regained my bearings and found the restaurant where we had agreed to meet.

My candidate was a tremendous disappointment! He was not only overweight, but he had a look that I could never find attractive. Our conversation was strained, to say the least. I politely pushed the date to an early conclusion and drove the half-hour back to my home. This little adventure took nearly two hours of my time. Then and there, I resolved never again to make an exception to my policy of meeting close to home — no matter how good my prospect sounded on the phone!

CHAPTER 11

Recognizing the Right Match for You

Love is a beautiful thing. Love has the power to move mountains and make the gloomiest day seem bright. When you find it, you can be overwhelmed with the pure joy of the emotion. When you can't find it, you can sink into despair — wondering if you will ever have a feeling that talks to your heart. We all have our own vision of love, and how we feel when we're in love or have it in our life.

I suspect that there is more than one person in this world that you can be happy with. They may even be completely different types of people. Beneath the superficial personality traits on the outside, there is a person inside. You will quickly know how you feel about obvious physical characteristics (and you could change the way he dresses...), but it's what's inside that matters in a long-term relationship.

You will meet a lot of people and, hopefully, you will want to see some of them again. Some candidates will stand out — the chemistry will be there and they qualify in other ways as well. Others will be maybes. The maybes are the most troublesome. You want to get to know them, but how much time do you invest in movies, dinners, and so on before you edit that particular candidate off of your list?

You *will* find someone to love — the question is merely *when* you will find that person.

How will you know when you have found the love of your life? There are some sure signs that you have met the man or woman who is right for you. Keep your eyes wide open, and be patient. The man or woman of your dreams is waiting to meet you!

THE FOUR KEYS TO A LASTING RELATIONSHIP

Life can seem to speed by when you are with someone you really enjoy. Finding a person you can love with all your heart and soul, and who loves you as much as you love them, is probably the greatest feeling you will ever experience in this life.

As a result of my seminars, I have spoken to many people about life and love. Based on these discussions, as well as others with friends and acquaintances, I have found that there are just four areas where we communicate with and relate to someone. This seems so simple, but it has been a tremendous help to me in evaluating past and present relationships.

The first way we relate to others is **intellectually.** This area of communication includes the areas of intelligence, education, attitudes and ways of thinking and approaching situations. Have you ever felt uncomfortable speaking to someone who was more highly educated than you — perhaps a research scientist or a college professor? If you are not at approximately the same intellectual level as your date, it is likely that you will not enjoy their company. Attitudes can be particularly important. We all like people who are like us.

The second way we relate to others is **physically.** This includes sexual chemistry, physical attractiveness, energy level and athletic ability. If you are a low-energy person, and you are happy to be that way, you might not get along very well with someone who always wants to be doing something. You may find someone grows more attractive as you get to know them. Sexual attraction is the ultimate in intimacy and communication.

The third way we relate to others is **emotionally.** This area includes how we feel and how we express and share our feelings. Your needs and the way you express your emotions may not be exactly the same, but the couples who succeed in this area are those who can understand and relate to one another emotionally.

The fourth way we relate to others is **spiritually.** This includes everything from traditional religious beliefs to humanitarian philosophies and ideals. All of us have personal belief systems and, while you don't have to agree on every little thing to have a successful relationship, you should agree on your most basic beliefs. If you don't respect your prospect's attitudes, or the way they treat other people, then you have a future problem on your hands. How can you continue to love someone you don't respect?

I believe that, in most close friendships, we master at least three out of four of these different ways of relating to each other. When we share and relate in all four areas, then we have a truly outstanding relationship. I can look back at failed relationships or other close encounters of the personal kind and see that one or more of these elements was missing. Like a table with one or two short legs, the relationship was weak or unbalanced. Naturally, there were problems, disappointments and lack of communication.

When you are involved in a relationship, you often can't see the whole picture. However, by looking at your relationship using these four standards of communication, you will see the big picture. If a part is missing, you can try to integrate that area into your relationship. If you try and fail, at least you will know before you have invested too much in the relationship, and you can take steps to go on. Don't rationalize that it will be okay, or that it will get better over time. We're talking fundamentals here, and fundamentals don't change — yours or your prospect's.

Beth was interested in John from the moment she met him. He definitely fit her profile: tall, good looking, smart, financially upper-end — and he clearly wanted to please her. A former football player, he still had an excellent physique and a strong, handsome face. His Armani suits draped beautifully from broad shoulders, and he wore all his clothes with a casual, relaxed style, obviously comfortable with himself. This was not a man who needed to impress anyone. Formerly a lawyer, he had long since founded his own successful transit business and worked long hours to keep it thriving. In his spare time, he loved to play tennis. What could possibly go wrong?

Early on, Beth became aware that, in spite of his significant success, this was a man who had worked his way up. The expensive clothes could not entirely hide his rough edges, and he lacked some of the finer social graces. The "can do" approach that had served him well in business was not always appropriate in a social setting. What had worked just fine as a date became an issue when they began to discuss a future together.

Beth had to take a hard look at her relationship with John. Despite his obvious intelligence, they lacked an essential connection both intellectually and spiritually. The fact that they matched beautifully on physical and emotional levels was not enough. Eventually, they agreed to part.

It's not easy to make these choices, but there is very little benefit in continuing a relationship with a person who is not right for you.

Relationships take time. Some evolve faster than others but, when they don't work out, we all wish that we could have seen the writing on the wall sooner. As you get to know someone new, continue to ask questions and look for evidence that your prospect meets your needs and seeks the same or similar goals in a relationship.

Use your notebook. Set up a page with these four categories and note how you relate to each other in each. Be honest. It pays to take a very good look at the way you and your partner function in each of these four ways of communicating before you commit.

GIVE IT TIME

When I first met Richard, the man who is now my husband, there was no big clue that he was the one for me. My first impression of him

CHAPTER 11: RECOGNIZING THE RIGHT MATCH FOR YOU

was only so-so. I came away from that first walk on the beach with him thinking that he seemed like a nice guy — faint praise, I suppose. My initial feeling was that he might be a bit too straight and narrow for someone of my artistic bent and eclectic tastes. Although he dressed casually enough, his clothes were so very well pressed, and his shoes matched a little too well.

I was already seeing two men at that time. Although I enjoyed them both, I didn't view either as having long-term potential. There was enough of a "maybe" in my evaluation of Richard that I kept him on my list for a follow-up date. Boy, am I glad I did!

While you are getting to know your new acquaintance, keep an open mind. Look for clues that will tell you if this relationship is one that might last. Take your time, and be open to letting that person into your life. This may seem contradictory, but you need to be both cautious and optimistic. At the same time, you have to be able to recognize when there are basic flaws in your relationship, and when you should call it quits and move on with your search.

If you have been out on several dates, and something is missing — perhaps one of the four ways that we relate with each other, such as the physical or intellectual attraction or interest — then test the waters to see if there is a chance that you can make the relationship complete. If not, you have to move on. There are simply too many others out there hoping to meet someone like you.

If you are persistent, you will find the man or woman of your dreams. You'll just have to stay motivated, optimistic, even tenacious.

It took me two years to find my husband through the personal ads. The first time I used the ads, it took about six months of marketing, screening and interviewing before I met a man I was interested in. This developed into an exclusive, six-month relationship. After I broke off that relationship, I didn't feel that I had wasted six months. I was happy, however, that I hadn't invested more.

I went back to the ads for another six months, give or take a month or two. So, you can see that each time I used the personal ads, it only took me about six months to meet someone really special. When I met Richard, he was recently separated, and new to the personal ads. He called my ad and two others. He never used the personal ads again. I have often thought that, if I hadn't had an ad running right then, we might have never met!

Sometimes you will hit it off with someone right when you meet. We have a term in real estate called "curb appeal." Curb appeal refers to a house that looks great from the street — one that you fall in love with the moment you arrive.

Remember The Executive who later married? He had curb appeal — very handsome, great voice, a real gentleman. I was immediately swept off my feet. Although I dated The Engineer for six months, he did not have curb appeal. However, once I got past his exterior, I discovered a wonderful man with a very beautiful inner self.

In real estate, when you pre-qualify a buyer and select houses to view, you already have the floor plans. Similarly, with the personal ads, when you pre-qualify your prospects, you will in essence have their floor plans — the floor plans to their inner selves. If you hit it off with a prospect right when you meet and you have already pre-qualified them as someone you might like, this can be a great bonus.

Remember, Beth was not immediately enamored with the ski partner who is now her one and only. Interestingly, our first impressions of our partners were very similar — we thought they were just so-so. But since they were pre-qualified for traits important to us, a so-so rating was actually a very high score.

With Richard, each date was a discovery of how much we had in common and how comfortable we were together. Each new shared interest and value expanded our communication and brought us closer together.

Most of the time, the personal ad process will be discouraging. You have a great conversation with someone, you spruce up for your meeting, and your heart starts to beat a bit faster with anticipation. Then you meet, and not everything was as it had seemed. And sometimes you meet and everything goes great. You can't wait to hear back from your date, but he never calls. This happened to Beth and me more times that we care to remember. Sometimes you never know why you got edited off their list. Perhaps an old girlfriend resurfaced. It happens.

Don't get too upset about these outcomes. Many of these cases are close encounters, but something just wasn't right — whether you recognize it or not. Don't spend too much time worrying about what went wrong — just keep advertising, screening and interviewing. Keep working, keep trying. Don't give up! You only need to find one person who is right for you.

EVALUATE WHAT WORKS

Do you ever get the feeling that all the good ones are already taken and you are stuck with the leftovers? If you are anywhere near my age — I was forty-two when I started using the personal ads — you would rightly assume that most of the men you meet have already been married at least once. Does that make them failures or leftover goods? No matter who is to blame for their divorce, the question is, did they learn from their experience?

It is incredibly important for us to learn from our mistakes and move on. Maybe they are better people now. Maybe you are, too. Maybe you were all just with the wrong partners.

An interesting byproduct of preselecting for potential compatibility is that, when you do find someone you like, it's so easy to talk and communicate. Your chances of finding a kindred spirit are much greater.

Have you ever had difficulty talking to someone you care about? I know I have. With Richard, and with so many other success stories from the people taking my seminar, I have noted an interesting coincidence. When you are with someone you have a lot in common with, you become a better communicator. Maybe some of the problems you had in the past were because you were with the wrong person. Meanwhile, keep evaluating your new friendships while you continue to place ads, screen, and interview.

If you have been running ads for some time and you aren't attracting the kinds of candidates that you want, try a new approach. Can you take a different slant or select new key words? Is your voice mail message positive in tone and in expressing your situation? Are you being too strict, or not strict enough in your interviews?

Consider what you are doing wrong and work to correct it. If you are uncertain, ask a close friend to read your ad and listen to your voice mail message. It is often much easier for someone else to identify a problem or bring a fresh approach.

On the other hand, what is working for you? Perhaps you are getting a lot of interest in your ad, and people are leaving you messages. If that is the case, then build on your success in those areas and try to extend this success into the other areas of the personal ad process. Are there other publications in your area that you could also be using? Continue to refine the parts that work to further narrow your responses to exactly the people you are seeking.

CHEMISTRY MAY SURPRISE YOU

There are many myths surrounding romantic love, and love at first sight is one of them. It's not that it never happens. It happens just enough to keep the myth alive. My concern is that believing that lightning will strike can distract you from recognizing the long-term love you might have with someone whose physical presence does not sweep you off your feet. At one time or another, we have all been attracted to a stranger, but does that make us compatible as life-mates?

It's like the old Judy Collins song, "I've looked at life from both sides now." Looks are important. If someone disgusts you, by all means go on to the next voice mail message. But looks aren't everything. It's quite possible that the perfect person for you is not drop-dead gorgeous.

It sounds disloyal to say that Beth and I were not swept off our feet by the men we came to love through the personal ads. Let me make this perfectly clear — they are attractive men. But chemistry was not our first order of relating. We got to know them first.

At the risk of embarrassing Beth, myself, or even you the reader, Beth and I both feel that we have never, ever had more passionate and satisfactory intimate relationships than we now have with men who did not initially set our hearts to pounding. Fortunately, that came later!

You can interview and analyze all you want, but there is no substitute for just letting a relationship evolve. Don't rush. Someone may meet all of your goals and still not be the right person for you. Similarly, a person may not meet each and every one of your goals but, as you get to know them, your desire to be closer grows. They may turn out to be the one you truly care for.

It is not always the best and the brightest people who have the greatest success in life. IQ alone is no determinator. It's the person with commitment and desire who achieves the greatest success in life. That's why I believe that attitude and self-concept are much more important than a person's job or existing assets. You can lose your job or your assets, but very few people lose themselves.

People don't really change as they get older — they just become more like themselves.

What I am saying is, don't rely too much on chemistry. If the spark isn't there to begin with, but you like this person, give it time. You may be surprised!

Our society still responds to beauty and attractiveness. I believe that it can be a disadvantage to be too attractive — especially when you are growing up. People make certain assumptions about individuals based on how they appear. How often have you heard it said of a young person, "With their good looks, they will do just fine in life." As if nothing more were required!

How does this impact your selection of a mate? The point is to look deeper for content, and don't be fooled by the gloss. An attractive man or woman may parlay their looks into a successful stage, screen or modeling career. Good looks are certainly an asset, but what else does the person have going?

Chemistry is a two-way street. As you look for the man or woman of your dreams, it's important that you take a close look at yourself, too. Are you a nice person? What personal skills do you bring to a relationship? For chemistry to work its wonders, you have to do your part. Make a point of asking your date questions, and then asking them to expand on what they told you by saying something like "That's interesting. How old were you when that happened?" The truth is, people like to talk about themselves. When you facilitate this, you will make a more favorable impression with your date while learning more about them.

Finally, be generous. Learn the vital skill of letting the other person shine and look good. Have you ever done that for a friend or co-worker? You deliberately bring up a topic or subject that you know is of interest to them because you know they excel at it. Learn to do this with the people you meet — especially later, as you get to know them and find yourself in groups of people. This simple technique is not only common consideration and caring, but it will definitely encourage them to express themselves.

KEEP YOUR OPTIONS OPEN

If you are really interested in someone after the first few dates, you will find yourself spending more and more time together. Before you know it, you are spending most weekends and often much of the week together.

This is, of course, a natural progression. However, as the chemistry between you and your prospect becomes increasingly intoxicating, be careful not to lose sight of your goals. You should continually evaluate the relationship with an eye toward its long-term possibilities.

As you build your relationship, remember, unless you are engaged to marry and have set the date, you're still available. I feel strongly that, until you actually marry, you should continue to advertise and meet people through the personal ads.

Why? How often have you been filled with regret that, not only has a relationship ended, but you have no other options? Why not keep your options open?

Beth is now dating a wonderful man she met through the personal ads. They clearly adore each other — frequent ski trips, theatre performances and lots of private time together. I wouldn't be at all surprised if Beth told me tomorrow that they have decided to marry.

From time to time, Beth still places an ad just to see who might call. Occasionally, she even meets her callers for coffee or lunch. Far from taking away from her current association, these meetings remind her just how much she enjoys their special relationship.

I don't find that to be unethical or underhanded. It's smart. If, for some reason, things don't work out between Beth and her ski partner, there are several outstanding gentlemen she can call immediately.

Just interviewing or meeting with your best prospects is no different from having coffee with someone you met at work. If Beth finds that she is very interested in one of these new prospects, she would have to evaluate her relationships and decide what is best for her.

THE DOCTOR

Here was another guy who sounded great on the phone. He was a retired cardiologist, and we seemed to have a lot in common. He described himself as looking like a former football player. In my imagination, I pictured a man who was burly, but fit. Our conversation was fantastic and we agreed to meet.

When I first laid eyes on The Doctor, I almost panicked! When he told me that he looked like a former football player, he meant that he was big and fat! Thank goodness, I recovered my composure long enough to at least sit down and say a few words. Our conversation picked up right where we had left off on the phone, and he actually began to become attractive in my eyes.

We went out a few times and became good friends. It turned out that the Doctor was a very nice person — a generous and interesting man. I am glad I took the time to look past his exterior and get to know the real man within.

You are almost at the end of your journey. We have discussed all the steps involved in writing and placing your ad, recording your voice mail message, listening to your callers' messages, taking notes and prioritizing them. We have called the best candidates back, interviewed them, and arranged to meet some of them. We have discussed where and how to conduct your first meetings, and considered the signs to look for in your prospect that would indicate that he or she is right for you.

As this book comes to a close, it's time to reflect on what you have learned and look to the future. You are never through with the personal ad process until you are married or settled in a caring relationship. Only then can you claim success.

CHAPTER 12

To Your Success!

As you have seen, the personal ads are an effective way to meet the kinds of people you are looking for. If you are willing to invest some time and effort in the process, you will be successful beyond your greatest expectations. I know this because of the many success stories I have heard, and continue to hear, from my many friends, clients, and the many men and women who have taken my seminar and who have used the personal ads to find lifelong love and companionship.

How you use the personal ads is entirely up to you. Your approach may be much more casual or relaxed than mine. That's okay — use the ads any way you wish. Perhaps you will use them only occasionally, to supplement the people you are already meeting or dating. If phone interviewing is not enjoyable for you, use my advice about meeting at your convenience to save time and energy. Do your screening when you meet.

By all means, adapt and change the techniques I discuss in this book to suit your personal style and your needs.

I do strongly believe that the unique aspect of the personal ad process is the opportunity to meet exactly the right person for you. If that is your goal, a concerted effort similar to the organized methods described here is an effective and efficient way to market, screen, and pre-qualify candidates for your future life mate.

Hopefully my approach will serve as a general guideline and set of suggestions to help you develop your own strategy. Create your own, personal approach. If you do evolve my ideas and recommendations to develop your own approach, there are just two things that I request of you: (1) Use common sense, and (2) Keep a record of all calls. These steps are for your own safety and security.

THE ART OF THE POSSIBLE

You may have noticed that some of my advice on how to proceed seems contradictory on the surface. One example is my advice to be skeptical when you interview, but remain open-minded. These ideas are not mutually exclusive — look for balance. Do be cautious when you agree to meet people and when you begin to develop a relationship with them. But also keep an open mind when you consider what might work for you. There may well be a person or lifestyle that is good for you that you hadn't really anticipated.

Expect disappointment while remaining optimistic. Most of the people you meet will probably be near-misses. But since you kept the meeting convenient for you and have not wasted a lot of time, it will be easier to keep a positive attitude and go on to the next possibility.

Although you will give your new acquaintance the benefit of the doubt, continue to assess your growing relationship. Be prepared to edit your list of companions to make room for new potential partners. Don't rush into exclusive relationships.

Men and women are frequently attracted to what is not good for them or what is unlikely to evolve into a lasting relationship. We're all guilty of this, but we can learn from our experiences. The right person isn't necessarily boring or dull like some medicine that tastes awful but will be good for you. Look past the surface of the people you meet. A foundation of respect and mutual concern may grow into a stimulating — even passionate — relationship.

However you choose to conduct your campaign, casually or highly organized, I cannot emphasize often enough that the opportunity to use voice mail to screen and pre-qualify your prospects makes personal ads particularly effective. Not only will the quantity of the people you meet increase, but the quality will increase, too. This will help you meet exactly the kind of people you wish to meet.

My goal was to marry if I could find the right man — one I could care enough about to weather the good times and the not-so-good times. I also reserved the right to not marry if that turned out to be the best outcome for me.

Although I didn't feel any urgency to find a man quickly, Beth and I did have one eye on the clock. We were well aware that we weren't getting any younger and that our options were not going to improve with time. Likewise, now is the best time for you to find your perfect mate through the personal ads. You can have an impact on your destiny. It's not easy, but it is efficient, effective, and free.

HAVE A BUDDY FOR MORALE AND SUPPORT

I am very grateful that I had the support of my friend Beth throughout the personal ad process. We were a great team, and we had a lot of fun.

The best part about having a buddy is that they can help keep you motivated and on top of your deadlines. It's also great to have someone to talk to about your interviews and dates.

During the time I worked the personal ads, I confided in very few people. Many people still think that personal ads are a little sleazy, or only for desperate people, so I simply didn't talk about it.

My mother was unaware that I used the personal ads, and it always amused me when she said, "You don't seem to have any trouble meeting men!" It wasn't until after I was engaged to marry Richard that I told my mother how I had met my husband-to-be.

Since I am now out of circulation, Beth rounded up a couple of friends to be her new partners. Personal ad buddies have a lot more

CHAPTER 12: TO YOUR SUCCESS!

interest in listening to your stories than the average person, who will quickly tire of hearing every detail of your ongoing saga.

Beth and her new buddies are all about the same age — late forties to early fifties, and they all live in the same area. They are attractive, smart, accomplished and, not surprisingly, they have met some great guys. Since their ages and locations are so similar, at times they receive calls from the same men.

Knowing that it often takes some time to get in touch, one gentleman left messages for Beth and her personal ad pals, Sharon and Amy. Beth was the first one to reach the caller. The interview went well, and they agreed to meet for cocktails at a nearby restaurant.

When Sharon and Amy heard about this arrangement, they wanted to go, too! Beth decided that it would be fun for everyone to get a chance to check out their caller at the same time, so she told them where and when they were to meet. Not one to take advantage of her caller, she graciously left him a message disclosing her plan.

When the three ladies reached the valet parking at the very tony restaurant, they were greeted by the hostess, who practically bounded from the entrance in her eagerness. She was as excited as the patrons at the bar who had seen the goings on in the restaurant.

Seated at a table for four was the gentleman. On the table were two open bottles of white wine, four wine glasses, along with fresh flowers and a heart-shaped box of chocolates for each lady. This gentleman definitely scored major bonus points for style and flair! They all had a lot of fun, and each of the ladies found their host charming and attractive.

While I'm not recommending group dates of the sort that Beth, Sharon and Amy shared, it's great to have the encouragement and support of a good friend as you search for the person of your dreams. It can make the process a lot more fun, and even your disappointments can become a lot less painful for you.

Please don't date out of boredom. It's not fair to the other person, who may come to rely on your company or have false expectations. Find ways to enrich your own life. Perhaps a seminar, adult education, an art appreciation course or walking with a friend. You will benefit from these efforts and, later, when you do meet someone of interest, you will bring more to the new relationship. Plus, there are no messy loose ends to tie up.

Don't use the personals as time killers. Make space in your life for new and better opportunities. Using the personal ads can provide opportunities for you to grow as a person, but they shouldn't provide your only social outlet. Continue to review how well you communicate in the four areas we talked about: intellectually, physically, emotionally and spiritually. Continue to discuss your life goals with your friends as well as the people you meet.

All this is time invested in yourself — in your future.

Even though you will prequalify the people you meet through the personal ads, there is still much to learn about a new friend. The person who said that they plan to marry really does mean that. However, don't assume that means they are ready to marry *you*.

It's so easy to make assumptions, as I did with Mr. Wonderful, with the polo player — even with The Engineer, who I met through the personal ads. Your friends can give you insights on your prospects, but your best defense is a thorough and straightforward interview. Hopefully you will learn from my lessons and do even better.

CHANGE AND EVOLVE YOUR GOALS AND AD

Take the time to periodically assess your progress. Are you still getting a reasonable number of calls, or have they tapered off? Are you meeting the kind of men or women that you have targeted, or do they seem to consistently fall short of the mark? Are you still having fun?

CHAPTER 12: TO YOUR SUCCESS!

If you answered "no" to any of these questions, it is time to change your approach.

Are your goals still accurate and appropriate? It's very natural for us to have a certain concept of ourselves and the people we want to meet when we first launch our advertising campaign. It is just as natural for this concept to change as we interview and meet prospects. For example, you may have originally specified that callers should be between forty and fifty-five years of age. However, after interviewing and meeting several men in their fifties, you may decide that you prefer men in their forties. If this is the case, do not hesitate to modify your advertisement and voice mail message accordingly.

Take the time to review, edit and re-write the characteristics of your ideal prospect. As your list evolves, you will come closer to defining what you really want out of life and out of a relationship. This is as much a process of personal growth as it is of finding a partner. I will always believe my list is what really brought Richard into my life. It helped me recognize him.

Perhaps your ad is too conservative or too wild. You may find that your callers are dull workaholics who have little time available to spend having fun. If so, and this is not the kind of person you want to meet, take a close look at your ad. Perhaps it should be modified to attract a different kind of caller. Conversely, if your ad appeals to people who are too party-oriented for your taste and you would prefer a more sober audience, review your ad and revise it with an eye to the kind of person you really want to attract.

Your personal ads and voice mail messages can be modified relatively quickly and easily. Take full advantage of your voice mail system's capabilities and experiment with a wide variety of ads.

Try something different one week and take careful note of the reaction. Different things attract different people. You may be a brunette, tall, smart, athletic career woman who would like to settle down and raise a family. In one ad, you might emphasize your athletic, long legs. In another, you might pitch your interest in starting a family. In still another ad, you could lean on your independence and career orientation. Although all these traits are very much a part of you, each ad will draw responses from distinctly different audiences. The combinations are endless. Keep experimenting with different approaches and combinations of your most interesting features.

If an approach isn't working for you, change it. You can greatly improve the probability of your success by being flexible. Above all, don't abandon the personal ad process just because you aren't getting the results you hoped for.

Take a close look at your personal goals and ensure that your ad and voice mail message are reflective of those goals. If you aren't sure what changes to make, ask a close friend to help.

SALLY'S SUCCESS

Sally was a student in my very first seminar. She had been divorced for sixteen years when she attended our session. During this time, she had dated and pretty much done the same things everyone else does to meet people. After many years of trying with limited success, she was ready to give up. She realized that, at fifty-seven, her chances of meeting Mr. Right were becoming increasingly slim.

A spirited and independent lady, Sally was by no means depressed by this prospect, just resigned. She enjoyed a comfortable lifestyle, and she respected success and achievement in a man or woman. Her ad read:

> **Classy lady, blond, North Coastal, energetic, independent, enjoys casual and outdoors to elegant and sophisticated. Stimulating conversation a plus. Please reply same, gentlemen ages 50+.**

It wasn't long after Sally attended my seminar that I heard through a mutual friend that she had met a great guy through the personal ads. A few weeks later I was invited to a party Sally and her new friend would be attending. When I arrived, Sally took me aside and said, "He's coming. He's meeting me here and I want to introduce you to him."

When I saw a very handsome man arrive and move quickly to Sally's side, I was thrilled — as if it were my own date. Dean was definitely attractive, with the build of a man much younger than his sixty-four years. I enjoyed meeting him, and I listened to his story intently. He was recently divorced, and he had elected to move to our area to start all over again. Job and career were of no concern to him — he was retired and had plenty of projects and interests to keep himself busy.

He went on to tell me that, based on his observations of friends and associates, it was his opinion that the type of woman who would be best for him was one in his own age bracket. He knew that he could attract the interest of younger women, but he felt strongly that a relationship with a younger woman would not last. He had found that the kind of women he sought didn't hang out in bars or in any other place where he could conveniently meet them. That's why he had turned to the personal ads.

Dean called on only three ads, including Sally's, and he met all three women. While he didn't hit it off with the other two, with Sally he found his match. They are now constant companions — enjoying all that a life of leisure has to offer.

THE MAN OF MY DREAMS

When I received Richard's message, I was not exactly impressed. I liked the tone of his voice and his energy, but he seemed a little smooth, pat, maybe slick. I was definitely aware that he was selling himself to me. His telephone prefix was in an area that I considered less desirable, but he did mention owning his own home. Up to now, the message was a "maybe."

Then Richard mentioned his exciting career in the lending and mortgage business, and the fact that he found it to be challenging and rewarding. His voice carried a genuine enthusiasm I could relate to, although I was concerned that our careers were too similar and subject to the same economic factors.

The telephone interview was okay, but not great. I learned that he was recently divorced, worked long hours and, good news — he had no children. By the time I spoke with Richard, I was starting to get a bit relaxed in my interviewing techniques, and I didn't ask him many questions. I was becoming a little bored with some of my personal ad "dates," and my level of enthusiasm was not high. Still, Richard fit my parameters closely enough that I felt I should at least do a look-see. We agreed to meet at a cafe near my home.

Although he looked nice enough, I must admit that my first impression was not great. He was too straight arrow — too vanilla. We talked, and I was impressed with his ability to discuss a wide range of subjects. By the end of our meeting, I could tell that he wanted to see me again. However, I was already dating two other men and was chairing a big volunteer fundraising program. This was in addition to the demands of my busy real estate career and the time I devoted to raising my children. With all these things on my agenda, I didn't see how I would be able to fit Richard in.

He called the following week to ask me out for a movie that weekend. His timing was good, since my schedule wasn't overly booked yet, and I agreed to go. I was surprised that he enjoyed the movie as much as he did. We saw an art film — not the kind most men prefer. I put Richard on my "B," or "backup" list. We went out a few more times — once to a museum reception with dancing to follow. He clearly enjoyed the modern art, and we had a wonderful evening dancing under the stars. There was more to this man than I had first noticed.

There was no one defining event that changed my mind about Richard — he just grew on me. At some point I woke up and realized how much I enjoyed spending time with him, and that I wanted to get to know him better. I accepted a date to drive up the coast for lunch and then dinner. The day was beautiful — sapphire, crystal-clear sky, effervescent waves kissing the shoreline, warm sun on our shoulders — the kind of day that makes me remember why I moved from Michigan to California those many years ago. We had a marvelous time, and it was hard to say good night.

For many months, we played the dating game. I introduced Richard to many of my friends, and they all adored him, too. Gradually, I learned more about his background, even meeting his parents when they visited. I was reassured to see how fit and healthy they were, mentally and physically. I firmly believe that you can learn a lot about a person by meeting their family.

Richard's upbringing was different from mine, but our fundamental beliefs and attitudes were similar. I became aware of his kind heart and generous spirit by the way he treated me, the way he described his choices in life, how he felt about change and the challenges he had faced over time. I found myself respecting his judgments and appreciating his opinions.

When the chemistry between us kicked in, it was a wonderful gift. I almost resented that Richard had not shared this aspect of himself with me sooner! What a wonderful surprise it was to fall in love with someone I liked, respected and truly enjoyed.

With any marriage, you take chances. No one has a crystal ball. My greatest concern was simply to get it right, to not divorce again. And more, to be happy in fundamental ways — mentally, physically, emotionally and spiritually. I thank my lucky stars that I took the time to get to know this man. We have been married a year now, and our love just grows and grows. Richard is the man of my dreams.

This is what life is all about — to find a love you enjoy day by day. It's the feeling my mother had for my father — the kind of love that lasts forever. I truly am a lucky woman!

IF AT FIRST YOU DON'T SUCCEED

It still amazes me how many people try the personal ads and then drop out. This is unfortunate, because I know first-hand how well the ad process works. You may be discouraged with your initial results, but you must realize that it takes time. It took me two years, and there were periods during which I, too, dropped out of the ads. If you stay with the efficient approach outlined in this book, and only meet at your convenience, it's easier to maintain your optimism. Look at every close encounter as an indication that quality people are out there, reading your ad, wanting to meet you.

Ultimately, it's your choice whether to accept responsibility for your life and take action to improve your future — or just wait and see what happens. Are you willing to work harder? It's your choice.

Life is like running a marathon. You don't just wake up one day and decide to run twenty-six miles that afternoon. It takes training and a lot of hard work. It takes hard work and effort to create and maintain a relationship and to be deserving of a good relationship, too. Train yourself to be ready.

As an artist, I created some very fine works. Like many artists, I was reluctant to promote my work — I was convinced that the world should recognize my obvious talent and come to me. It didn't take me long to realize that the world was not going to beat a path to my door. Today, many pieces of my artwork hang in public buildings and reside in prominent personal collections. They didn't get there by themselves. I had to go out and present myself, as well as my art.

Years later, when I started out in real estate, I had to decide whether to affiliate with a large or small office. A big office seemed intimidating, with all the bustle of activity and the competition. I knew I would be most comfortable in a small office, and I discussed my decision with a close friend. She told me, "Mary, why not go with the biggest, busiest office? Won't you learn more from them?"

She was right on target. You have to put yourself out there and accept the challenge. The owner of the large office had a great training program, and it was absolutely the best place to learn about sales, marketing, follow-up, and how to pre-qualify prospects. Can you guess the most important thing he taught me? Try harder. There is no secret. No short cut. No easy way out. If you really want something, you have to be willing to work for it.

Are you willing to make a commitment to your future happiness?

Personal ads may be free, but they are work! If you are looking or waiting for a free lunch, then I wish you luck! Save this book and read it again in five years. However, if you are serious about finding a mate to share the rest of your life with, then try harder. It may take months, it may take years. But, if you work hard, you *will* succeed.

My goal in the personal ads was to meet more eligible men. Men of quality whom I would know in advance held similar beliefs and goals to mine. Therefore, my approach to the personal ads was like my approach to real estate or any endeavor I might wish to succeed at. Create goals and be efficient in seeking progress and results.

If something or someone is not right, change it or go on. This attitude may seem harsh — even cold, but you will have better results and save time if you let your heart and emotions follow, instead of leading. I tried following my heart, and took a few wrong turns. This was fine — even appropriate — when I had my whole life ahead of me, and much to learn. But now I wanted to get it right.

It wasn't always easy for me to keep the rational approach. Relationships are distracting, and we enjoy them on many levels. But I was determined to approach relationships as a foreign language, examining the pieces and elements that work and applying them to myself and to my future.

There were times when I chose to stay home rather than encourage a relationship that I knew was not quite right for me. You may wish to be more flexible in how you spend your time. But I felt that curling up with a good book was actually more appropriate than a movie with a man I had no potential with.

As a businesswoman, I didn't want to waste my time, energy, and emotional reserves trying to nurture the wrong relationship again and again. There were times when my feelings were hurt and perhaps I disappointed and hurt others. I hope not. I always tried to be fair and never give false hopes to another person.

My tools were simple — I hope that they now are clear to you. Identify what you want, and what you have to contribute. Stay focused on your parameters but remain open-minded. Be prepared to screen, meet with disappointment, and edit out the near-misses. It will take time and effort, but the reward is great — a life-mate you will enjoy. Forever.

Regardless of your age and experience, I hope you will find some value in my story and my lessons. Whether you view this as your first chance or your last chance, we all want to get it right. No one seeks failure or divorce. Your investment will be time and energy — the ads are free. And the opportunity to meet the right person is the chance of a lifetime — your lifetime.

It worked for me. It worked for Beth, for many of my seminar students and for untold numbers of others. It can work for you.

Nice girls can — and men can, too.

CHAPTER 12: TO YOUR SUCCESS!

TALKING HEARTS ORDER FORM

Nice Girls Can (Men Can, Too)

may also be ordered from your local bookstore.

NICE GIRLS CAN (MEN CAN, TOO)

Paperback Edition, 156 pages $14.95

HOW TO FIND YOUR PERFECT LIFE MATE

Audio Cassette Seminar Program $16.95

Please send: _____ Book(s) @ $14.95 each   total: $ _____

_____ Cassette(s) @ $16.95 each   total: $ _____

Add $2.50 Shipping: $ _____

Total Amount Enclosed: $ _____

Charge my: ☐ Mastercard   ☐ VISA   ☐ AMEX

Account # _____

Exp. Date _____

Signature _____

To: _____

Address: _____

City: _____ State: _____ Zip: _____

Make checks or money orders payable to:
Talking Hearts Press
1155 Camino Del Mar #148
Del Mar, CA 92014 (619) 794.7980

Allow 4-6 weeks for delivery. California Residents add applicable sales tax.

TALKING HEARTS ORDER FORM

Nice Girls Can (Men Can, Too)

may also be ordered from your local bookstore.

NICE GIRLS CAN (MEN CAN, TOO)

Paperback Edition, 157 pages $14.95

HOW TO FIND YOUR PERFECT LIFE MATE

Audio Cassette Seminar Program $16.75

Please send: _____ Book(s) @ $14.95 each   total: $ _____

_____ Cassette(s) @ $16.95 each   total: $ _____

Add $2.50 Shipping: $ _____

Total Amount Enclosed: $ _____

Charge my: ☐ Mastercard   ☐ VISA   ☐ AMEX

Account # _____

Exp. Date _____

Signature _____

To: _____

Address: _____

City: _____ State: _____ Zip: _____

Make checks or money orders payable to:
Talking Hearts Press
1155 Camino Del Mar #148
Del Mar, CA 92014 (619) 794.7980

Allow 4-6 weeks for delivery. California Residents add applicable sales tax.

SEMINARS & SPEAKING ENGAGEMENTS

Mary Hale welcomes the opportunity to speak to groups, sharing her insightful, often amusing story, practical approach and inspirational guide.

Talks from the Heart include:

HOW TO FIND YOUR PERFECT LIFE MATE

THE POWER OF PERSONAL CHOICE

DISCOVER THE BENEFITS OF VOLUNTEERING

EVALUATING AND ENHANCING RELATIONSHIPS

For more information,
contact
Talking Hearts Press
(619) 794.7980
1155 Camino Del Mar #148
Del Mar, CA 92014

Photo © H. Montgomery Drysdale